THE POWER OF A PARTNER

THE POWER OF A
PARTNER

Creating and Maintaining Healthy Gay and Lesbian Relationships

Richard L. Pimental-Habib, Ph.D.

los angeles | new york

MANUFACTURED IN THE UNITED STATES OF AMERICA.

THIS TRADE PAPERBACK ORIGINAL IS PUBLISHED BY ALYSON PUBLICATIONS,
P.O. BOX 4371, LOS ANGELES, CALIFORNIA 90078-4371.
DISTRIBUTION IN THE UNITED KINGDOM BY TURNAROUND PUBLISHER SERVICES LTD.,
UNIT 3, OLYMPIA TRADING ESTATE, COBURG ROAD, WOOD GREEN,
LONDON N22 6TZ ENGLAND.

FIRST EDITION: OCTOBER 2002

02 03 04 05 06 a 10 9 8 7 6 5 4 3 2 1

ISBN 1-55583-632-1

CREDITS
COVER PHOTOGRAPHY BY DIGITAL VISION.
COVER DESIGN BY MATT SAMS.

For John,
he of the biggest heart and kindest soul

CONTENTS

Part Three: Therapy

ACKNOWLEDGMENTS

An ancient Native American prayer claims, "The Creator never made anyone different without giving them something special." I am grateful to count among my friends and acquaintances a wonderfully diverse group of special, talented people. They have encouraged me throughout the writing of this book and beyond, indeed through all my creative efforts—past, present, and no doubt, future. I especially send heartfelt appreciation to Ginger, Peg, Rich, Janis, Dana, Tracy, Owen, Paul, Larry, and Chuck for their valuable contributions and support.

Also, my thanks to...

The many couples who over the years have allowed me to join their brave journeys, and all the single individuals who've sought my help in preparing their inner Cupid. We can all learn from each other, and my experiences with my clients have enriched me beyond measure.

Deidre Knight, my hardworking, watchdogging agent and dear friend.

Angela Brown, my talented editor at Alyson.

Eve, Bob, Bonita, and Buzzy for being a sweet family.

Lou, who would be proud.

And Julie, again and still.

INTRODUCTION

FINDING THE COURAGE TO LOVE

It is only with the heart that one can see rightly.
What is essential is invisible to the eye.
—Antoine de Saint-Exupéry

Lovers, life partners, significant others...siblings, mothers and sons, fathers and daughters...best friends, ex-lovers, colleagues. These are some of the relationships by which we define ourselves. They create the fabric of our lives. They illustrate the richness of our humanness, challenge our interpersonal skills, and give the world a window into who we are. For better or for worse, consciously or unconsciously, we are our relationships.

It is a very courageous act to love another, for loving requires vulnerability, an openness to the joys as well as the hurts. As adults, it's not always easy for us to allow ourselves to be vulnerable. Experience has often taught us to be guarded. And yet we're born with the capacity to love fully and unconditionally with an open, natural curiosity and, perhaps most importantly, an innate ability to be vulnerable. We enter this world with an energy and aliveness and resiliency that, over the years of pain and pleasure, through the hard knocks as well as the joys, will either increase or diminish. It's all part of the natural process of growth, of being in relationship with the other people also walking this planet. Courage, joy, hurt—they are all part of being human. And it is precisely when we develop the courage to feel the joy, to feel the hurt, and to make ourselves vulnerable to others that true internal transformation occurs.

But what about those times when we were courageous, took a chance, and lost? What do we do with past hurts? Do we carry our relationship war wounds around with us, like so much baggage to be unloaded onto the unsuspecting "next ex"? Or do we grow to understand that life's lessons take many forms and with each hurt comes the opportunity to heal and create for ourselves more aliveness, more openness than ever? Are we willing to learn from our mistakes—from our specific pasts, from our families, from our friends—and therefore bring to the table ever-increasing doses of wisdom, more opportunities to have fun, and some of that childlike love, curiosity, openness, and vulnerability with which we entered the world? How do we, as adults with our own personalized sets of baggage, learn to prepare fully and genuinely for healthy relationships?

Let's be clear about something: There is a world of difference between *wanting* a relationship and being *ready* for a relationship. Perhaps everyone at one time or another wants to be in a meaningful relationship—wants to give love and feel love returned, to know that they are important, *of worth*, to at least one other human being on the planet; to know that they *matter*. But *readiness* implies something more. Readiness requires a healthy dose both of awareness and the courage described above. It requires a commitment to engage in self-examination with rigorous honesty. Readiness implies that a person understand that he or she is a work in progress with strengths and weaknesses, and that any healthy relationship requires the courage—and *patience*—to lovingly embrace the ongoing process that is another human being.

Will we empower ourselves to choose the relationships

through which we in part define ourselves—the relationships that make life worth living? And will we treasure those relationships with all our hearts? We were born open to love, willing to learn, and with a zest for life. The rest is all about choice, honesty, and becoming ready. To quote Walt Whitman:

> *Afoot and lighthearted I take to the open road,*
> *Healthy, free, the world before me,*
> *The long path before me leading wherever I choose.*

A STARTING PLACE

Perhaps a good starting place for any discussion about relationships is the idea that relationships are organic entities—growing, developing, stagnating, dying, renewing. Some are affected by time and distance, and others are not. They are the living, breathing rewards for being a good friend, devoted son, or fabulous lover. And in this way they illustrate who we like to be, or perhaps how we'd like to see ourselves. And when betrayed, our relationships boldly mirror back to us those sides of ourselves that are unflattering and undesired. Without attention and nurturing, relationships wither. With love, respect, and vigilance, they thrive. Very often they confuse and confound us, much like we ourselves are sometimes confused about who we are, or what we want, or how to live well and find some degree of happiness with others.

In my experience working with individuals, couples, families, and groups, I've found that many commonly perceived "problems" could actually help people evolve, if only there were some sort of relationship manual to help them through the rough spots. People often need some kind of guide to let them know they are not the first ones to struggle with these relationship issues and certainly won't be the last. They need a guide to teach them how to communicate, even when they're angry; how to understand that it's natural for feelings about a partner to fluctuate and falter; how to first look inside oneself as a prelude to looking into healthier ways of being a couple; and how to *learn* from adversity. These are the issues people struggle with constantly. Single people want to know how to find a mate with whom to form a healthy relationship and thereby break old, unhealthy dating patterns. Partnered people want to know how to stay monogamous, or how to foster a healthy shift in their love for each other when monogamy isn't working. Those newly dating want to know when to pick out the china. And everybody wants to know they are loved.

In the heterosexual world, couples have the role models with which they were raised to find guidance and answers. These models are sometimes sufficient, healthy, and helpful, and sometimes not. (Many people I know, both gay and straight, consider the term *dysfunctional family* redundant.) In the gay world, however, lesbians and gay men were very rarely raised by other gay people. (Sort of shoots holes in the "recruitment theory" espoused by the religious right, doesn't it? We comprise only 10 to 15% of the population on average, no matter who raised us!) Therefore, gay role models are usually not found from within one's immediate family of origin. Sometimes healthy role models can be found in one's circle of friends and acquaintances. More often, however, a gay person's friends are struggling along too, doing the best they can and dealing with similar issues themselves.

Our "families" are made up of all sorts of relationships—past, present, and future—and all have an aspect that is strikingly universal: At one point or another, when it comes to understanding and navigating the murky waters of intimate relationships, we are quite often clueless. As a therapist, I hear

the same earnest and often desperate questions over and over:
Did I say the right thing? Have I done the right thing? Are we
headed in a healthy direction? Are we headed for disaster? Does
everyone hate their parents? How do other couples handle this?
Where's the manual to help us?!

What This Book Offers

I've written this book to provide something of a self-help
guide that uses the experiences of other gay men and lesbians
to help you through the rough spots, those deep and troubling
waters where others have dared to tread. Real-life stories culled
from my 15-year private practice—as well as from personal
experiences with friends and family—illustrate honestly and
openly many of the relationship topics most important to gay
and lesbian lives. Using a format that presents what works and
what doesn't, it's my hope that you'll be able to experience
three therapeutic fundamentals:

- I am not alone with my issues.
- There is hope for my relationship(s).
- Here are practical guidelines I can try myself (or that we
  can try together).

Learning from each other is really such a simple idea, a
common-sense approach to attaining a healthy and happy life.
Much of what you'll read in these pages is taken from the true
stories of other gay men and lesbians: couples and singles dealing with the same issues that you are in your relationships.
They share their successes and difficulties, what works for
them and what doesn't—it's all here to provide you with
healthy role models from whom to learn.

The first section, titled "Partners," covers a wide range of topics: finding a healthy monogamous relationship, dealing with an "open" relationship, staying friends with the ex, tending one's heart with care and nurturance in preparation for a new lover, learning the difference between love and lust, and understanding why we choose whom we choose. The second section, "Family and Friends," looks at issues surrounding different types of platonic friendships, family relationships, and work relationship as well as what's at stake in these relationships when one decides to come out as gay or lesbian. And in the third section, titled "Therapy," there is an extensive discussion about how to heal and move on after a loss, as well as several relationship meditations and commonly asked questions (with answers) that address additional topics of concern. The primary goal of this book is to help you—and your loved ones—understand what works well, and what doesn't, for gay and lesbian relationships of all kinds.

WE'RE ALL IN THIS TOGETHER

While family problems are certainly not the sole property of the gay and lesbian community, it is true that many gay men and lesbians struggle with the relationships they have with their parents, especially if they aren't out to them or not accepted by them. Gay parents face more societal and parenting challenges than heterosexual parents. Older generations of family members are often at a loss as to how they might grow to accept their gay offspring. Gay teens often have little or no guidance when it comes to issues such as commitment and loyalty and compromise. In this book, I cover all of these relationship issues too. And in so doing I present a crucial point: *In order for a community to be healthy and whole, it must have everyone on board.* It must include Mom, Aunt Rose, and Sis as well as our colleagues and best friends. We all come from family, and we all experience family, whether by blood or by design. And if it's true that "no man (or woman) is an island," then perhaps the way to guide a community toward health, healing, and cohesion is with the understanding that we're all in this together.

Since the relationship issues that perplex and overwhelm people from time to time certainly are not the monopoly of gay folks, this book is intended for straight people as well. If you change a pronoun here and there, then anyone from a family, in a family, or involved with other human beings on an intimate level will derive benefit from this book. So feel free to share the messages herein with your straight friends. Further, since gay people often struggle the most with heterosexuals when coming out, it's vitally important that straight people find and develop healthy ways of having relationships with gay people too!

Current estimates show that 10% to 15% of the American population identifies as either lesbian or gay, and that percentage rises significantly when bisexual and transgendered people are included. Demographically, gay Americans earn more, spend more, read more, travel more, dine out more, collect more art, and explore and use self-help or "alternative" forms of healing and therapy more often than heterosexual people. Countless gay people understand the value of therapy, and many 12-step and other counseling programs are geared specifically with them in mind. Because so many gays and lesbians keep struggling to understand and resolve their relationship issues, this book aims to provide needed guidance to a population eager to learn how to apply some of their hard-earned psychological savvy to improving their relationships.

Toward that end, most chapters in this book pose thought-provoking questions and new ways of thinking for you and your mate as well as your friends and relatives, and conclude with a related affirmation. A few chapters offer a user-friendly meditation so the reader can begin to experience some internal healing, centeredness, self-awareness, and growth right away.

Whether among family, friends, or significant others, we indeed have within us the ability and power to choose, develop, and maintain healthy relationships. And we must learn to treasure these relationships by committing to personal growth, rigorous honesty, and self-awareness. For these are the qualities of good self-esteem—for ourselves, for our partners, for our relationships, for our community. In the spirit of Walt Whitman, it is my hope that this book inspires you to do the work to get ready: to be willing to take risks, to learn to embrace vulnerability, and to commit to loving relationships with others by using the creativity, aliveness, and freedom within yourself. Let the journey begin!

PART ONE
PARTNERS

How do I love thee? Let me count the ways.
—Elizabeth Barrett Browning

Chapter

One

Love, Lust, and Healthy Relationships

I fell in love this week—five times.
—overheard at a bar

Ah, lust. Desire. Infatuation. Limerence. Love. Feeling *in* love. Unrequited love. Falling out of love. Searching for love.

It seems only fitting that a book about relationships begin with a discussion of love and its many incarnations and manifestations. Love is the popular topic of songs, novels, films and art. It drives people to act in ways unusual and sometimes unimaginable. It is agony, and it is exquisite pleasure. It can renew the spirit and break the heart. It makes us feel foolish and wonderful. It's much more *felt* than it can be described. And it is the intangible something that confuses and confounds on a daily basis.

When a young person eager to learn about life and love asks an adult how he or she will know when love strikes, the answer is undoubtedly, "You'll know it when you feel it." That's helpful? Love is a bit of a mystery, an intangible, and yet is the very foundation upon which we base lifelong relationships. Everyone wants to know what it is to feel love for another and to feel love returned. We pursue love vigorously and relentlessly. And all along the journey we learn about ourselves—our capacity for love, our desires, our lusts, our wants, and our needs. Where we feel incomplete, we learn to go about finding completion and filling the void.

The philosopher Houssaye said, "Tell me whom you love, and I will tell you who you are." And C.S. Lewis posed, "Why love, if losing hurts so much?" When we love another, does that say more about the other person or ourselves? And why would we ever in a million years dare to love again after a relationship has ended?

Do we love a person the way we love pizza, or cerulean blue, or our pets? So many of us bandy the word around so casually, as if it weren't one of the most profound, powerful, life-altering emotions known to humankind. Some people cannot say "I love you." Three simple words, or are they? When a friend of mine says, "I love you" to his father, his father responds, "OK."

When it comes to the significant relationships in our lives, what role does love play? What is the role of lust? Do you know the difference? As we begin a journey of greater under-standing about our relationships, it behooves us to heighten our self-awareness of all our feelings in general and of love in particular. For it is precisely our most intimate and intense levels of feeling that arise when we enter relationships, whether they are based on romantic love, familial love, parental love, sisterly/brotherly love, "friendly" love, or even the absence of love.

Perhaps love isn't really in the equation for you during this period of your life. Maybe it's all about lust. Many people I've known, when on the rebound from a love lost, enter a period in which their agenda is about the fulfillment of carnal desire, physical abandonment, and lust. Lots and lots of lust. Love? Forget about it. All they want is a good time. I call this the "just say yes" phase. Such a phase can be a perfectly healthy, natural, and even necessary stage of emotional healing and eventual growth.

Making Healthy Relationship Choices

We as gay people indeed form many kinds of unique, healthy, unconventional, and satisfying relationships. Not enslaved by strict social or familial guidelines to which we must conform, many gays and lesbians tend to create as we go. And creative we are! Now, where our mental health is concerned, here is the crucial part: We must internalize for ourselves the *rightness* of our relationships. We need to understand that no matter what type of partnership we desire or design, it is valid, it is OK, it is our own.

The heterosexual world has rituals to help shape and validate their love lives and romances—proms and weddings, for example. Even a divorce is a rite of passage that is thus far an institution designed only for heterosexual couples. The point is that the world acknowledges your relationship-related passages and stages if you're straight. How many gay people have parents who said, "Good for you, honey, you're gay! Let me help you learn about love!" Or, "I have just the man/woman for you—let me help you nurture your gay relationship." Or how about, "Let's throw you a commitment ceremony. We'll invite everyone! Your father will be so pleased!"

Instead, with a lack of social sanctions for gays comes the widespread and, unfortunately, widely accepted message that our gay and lesbian relationships don't count, can't work, and won't last. When we buy into these base pronouncements, we internalize all the wrong self-esteem messages: *My* relationships can't work because they're not heterosexual; *I* don't know how to make them last because no one's ever shown me; *my* relationships don't matter because they aren't legally or socially sanctioned. It's no wonder it becomes so easy, once we hit adulthood, to feel confused and clueless about which relationships are healthy for our individual and collective self-esteem, and which are not. How can we know?!

STEP I

The first step toward making healthy relationship choices is *not* to buy into negative messages about our ability to create and maintain loving, lasting, rewarding relationships if we so choose. We can have whatever kind of relationships we desire, all of which are valid, and no one has the right to judge our relationships, whether or not they are socially, legally, or religiously supported. Just as each individual is unique, the kind of relationship each person desires is also specific and unique, whether it is lust-filled, love-filled, both, or neither.

Our lives would be very different if as children we had been routinely and consistently given the message that we are empowered to love whomever we desire without the interference of prejudice. You're gay? Great! Now let's move past that and get to the relationship part, the part where you're taught how to have loving, healthy involvements with terrific people. Too often the emphasis on "same-sex relationships" is on the *same-sex* aspect, instead of on the *relationships* aspect, where it can do us some good.

Each person who wants to develop and maintain healthy relationships must make conscious, mindful choices regarding the romances, friendships, and acquaintances he or she surrounds him/herself with. Each choice is valid, and each is our own responsibility. So choose wisely! OK, so how do we do we do that?

STEP 2

I suggest to you the following: We do not get what we *want* or even what we may believe we *need*. We get what we are *ready* for. Big difference. Sometimes our wants and needs coincide with our degree of readiness, and sometimes they don't. We'll explore this idea more fully throughout the rest of this book, but for now I encourage you to begin by asking yourself the following four questions. Such simple questions, really, on the surface, but the answers are seldom given the kind of thoughtful attention they deserve.

- What do I want in a partner?
- What do I *need* from a partner?
- What am I able to offer another person?
- What kind of relationship do I honestly believe I'm ready for?

How well do you know yourself? Some of us keep repeating unhealthy behavior patterns by engaging in a flurry of unsatisfying encounters that feed into an ongoing stream of frustrations as we distract ourselves with the "busyness" of disappointing dates. If we were to become quiet with ourselves and thus become better connected with who we are and what we want, we could begin to break our unhealthy relationship patterns. We would then be able to replace these patterns with behaviors and internalized messages that support of our self-esteem.

So this next important step toward having healthy, honest, genuine relationships is to realize that you must first have a healthy relationship with *yourself.* If you are ready to learn certain lessons about yourself, and if you are paying attention, you will be presented with ample and repeated opportunities to actualize those lessons. This is a critical and essential point: *If you are ready, the opportunities will arise.* Some of these lessons may be difficult and seem hidden at first; some may be more obvious. Some may be in the form of a heartbreaking experience; some may be in the form of true love. But all have the potential of being richly rewarding, no matter what kind of relationship agenda you may have for yourself, or what stage of life you're in.

In the spirit of this book, the spirit of learning from each other's life experiences, I want to share with you the story of a friend of mine, Michael.

Michael spent 10 years with a whirlwind variety of sexual partners. On the one hand he was having a lot of fun; on the other he felt tremendous frustration and disappointment, both with his sexual partners and himself. He felt locked into a cycle, and as long as he remained on this merry-go-round, distraction filled his life. He was missing something he suspected he could find "out there"—something healthier and more satisfying. But in 10 years he hadn't gotten any closer to finding it. As Michael says:

> It felt OK for the first year or so. I was enjoying playing around—meeting new guys and having fun. But I realized I wasn't getting any younger and was still feeling a void. My pursuit of men was my way to try and fill the emptiness, my loneliness. I didn't know how else to go about filling it up.

Michael's story is not uncommon. It's so easy and natural to think that we need to look outside ourselves for solutions, when really all the answers are within. Once Michael learned to look inward and listen to himself, he began to gain perspective. He took stock, took responsibility—and took a breath!—and grew more in touch with his true needs and wants. After much personal-growth work and committed soul-searching, he became *ready* for a relationship of the type he'd been hoping for deep in the private corners of his heart. That's precisely when he met his new life partner. This was several years back, and they're still together today.

The important point is that whatever kind of relationship you're seeking, it can only be found (or created) when you become aware of what's going on internally. If your having multiple sexual partners is acting as the Band-Aid that's covering your loneliness and stunting your emotional growth, how can you know that without turning inward and listening to yourself? Or if you're in a long-term monogamous relationship but are miserable with that choice, it's only fair to you and your partner to get in touch with what's going on for you within. Only then can you realistically identify the issues involved and learn to make healthy life decisions.

A while back a young man came to my office with complaints of being "used by men" and feeling frustrated and "taken advantage of" by everyone he was dating. After some exploration, it became clear that while he was pursuing men to satisfy his lust, he was really quite lonely and wanted to feel loved. His sex partners were good matches for his libido but poor matches for the commitment-oriented, romantic side of his personality that desired more. Up until this point, his only venues for meeting men were bars and roadside rest areas, hardly places one can expect to be romanced.

Again, after learning to listen more clearly to his inner self, in particular to his heart, he was able to pursue socializing through venues where he met men who were looking for some of the same qualities he was, qualities he himself had to offer. He became *ready* for romance and therefore began making choices to satisfy both his drive for physical fun as well as ongoing emotional happiness.

We experience *what we are ready* to experience. How mindful are you of your walk through life, the choices you are making, and the reasons for your choices? How receptive are you to the lessons that are coming your way? Are you listening to yourself? How are you preparing yourself to realize your potential as a person who is ready to give and receive love? That's how a healthy, happy life happens: as we become ready for it.

FROM LIMERENCE TO LOVE

Once we enter an intimate relationship, our task shifts from *finding* to *maintaining*. It's important to remember that, much as an individual grows, so too does a relationship grow from one stage to the next. Early on, your relationship may be in the "honeymoon period," that time marked by limerence (also called infatuation) and that certain light-headed feeling that keeps you soaring with exciting thoughts of your boyfriend or girlfriend. Limerence, though, is built on mystery, on seeing the other person infrequently. Therefore, limerence declines over time and upon greater exposure to each other.

Some people find they are addicted to limerence itself, and they confuse feeling *in* love with feelings *of* love, and may not know how to go from the honeymoon period to deeper emotional intimacy. Once the limerence fades, which is natural and inevitable, they mistakenly believe that what they're no longer feeling is love itself, and they move on to the next person. These people are "limerence junkies." They've never felt a deeper level of connectedness with someone beyond the infatuation stage, so they haven't learned what love is, or how to make it last. Therapy can be extremely helpful to individuals stuck in the limerence stage.

If, however, a couple's feelings deepen as their relationship enters a period of greater emotional intimacy and bondedness, then often a kind of unique and personal fabric develops between them as they get to know each other better, understanding each other's likes and dislikes, personality quirks, moods, and so on. Learning more about each other requires honesty, trust, and vulnerability, and is an indication of a couple's willingness to allow their love to grow. The question then becomes, is each partner able to find happiness with the other person as they discover more about him or her?

So what about lust—is it lost in the face of growing love? Does a lasting commitment necessitate a diminished sexual enjoyment, just because the limerence fades? Can lust cohabit with love?

You bet it can! Who says you can't have it all? My wish for you is this: that together, as you travel the road of your relationship and endure both the joys and obstacles that are a necessary part of the relationship, you will appreciate new ways of not only loving each other but of maintaining a lustful ardor and physical expression that feel as if they surpass anything any other couple has ever known. Remember, we are a creative bunch. In our uniquely individual, wholly personal process of growth, let's commit to a creativity and love that celebrates exactly who we are and what we are capable of. Let's take the steps to be *ready* for something wonderful.

~

I am committed to knowing myself, my needs and desires.

~

I am committed to being true to myself.

~

I celebrate who I am!

Chapter

Two

Dating Choices: Echoes From the Past

Why love, if losing hurts so much?
—C.S. Lewis

As human beings we are motivated to form emotional and physical partnerships with other individuals for a number of reasons, and these reasons often relate back to an earlier time in life when important interpersonal impressions were being formed—impressions therapists call "introjects." Mom, Dad, an uncle, grandparent, sibling, best friend, worst enemy, distant cousin, teacher, scout leader, minister, childhood sweetheart—they can all play a role in forming our introjects, the unconscious guiding impulses from early life that, for better or for worse, help shape and define who we are attracted to.

So, when it comes to dating, we tend to choose people for both conscious and unconscious reasons. Small snippets of familiarity from the past catch our eye—or our heart—and we find ourselves drawn to someone who touches that place inside, a place usually well hidden from *conscious* thought and desire. You may be conscious of being attracted to hazel eyes, but it takes investigation of the unconscious to remember, for instance, having your very first crush on a schoolboy with hazel eyes; or even further back, perhaps the first eyes you saw as a newborn baby were—you guessed it—hazel.

This dynamic takes many forms: We may be drawn to someone with a wry sense of humor, or a certain sideways glance, or someone with remarkable organizational skills. We may find comfort in the way someone arches her brow. We may be attracted someone who is sensitive or daring, someone who has a demanding or meek personality, a chip on his front tooth, or a certain lilt to his walk. The list goes on and on, and everyone's list is unique. But whether we are conscious or unconscious of our attraction to certain characteristics in others, the *reasons* for our attraction can be found in some corner of our personal history. It could date back to when you were 9 minutes old, 9 months old, or 9 years old, but it's back there somewhere.

This is why we are comfortable with certain people more than others, why we react positively or adversely to a color or smell; why we favor long hair over short, or dark skin over light, and so forth. I once had a client who didn't understand the strong negative reaction she experienced when she was near someone wearing a black sweater. We discovered during regression therapy that as a child she was frequently beaten up by an older sibling who often wore black sweaters. She had blocked it from her conscious mind, so painful was the memory of that early life experience.

Awareness = Healthy Patterns

Whether we are interested in knowing the reason for each and every one of our attractions and emotional reactions is, of course, optional. When it becomes important, however, is when you've brushed up against a limitation or difficulty in your life, particularly in the arena of relationships, and you don't know why. For instance, you may be repeatedly drawn to people who are emotionally or physically abusive, and you don't know how to break that pattern. This is an example of when it becomes important to understand exactly which echoes from your past influence your relationship choices, and why. The reason may be obvious, or it may be hidden. But only then will you come to know what impulses and introjects you're up against and how to deal with them—how to break your destructive patterns, grow through old destructive choices, and create newer, healthier ones.

So, when we form relationships in adulthood, a healthy relationship can make all the difference in repairing old wounds. Likewise, an unhealthy relationship can cause further psychological and emotional damage, picking up where childhood left off. It's much harder to break old destructive patterns than it is to simply continue with what feels familiar, *even when the familiar is destructive.* This is why people who were physically abused in childhood often end up in adult relationships with batterers. It's familiar. It may be unhealthy, even to the point of being life-threatening, but it's *known.* And the known is always less frightening than the unknown. This, by the way, is a perfect and dramatic example of the need for entering a therapeutic process. Therapy can move information held in the subconscious into the realm of the conscious, thereby discharging it of its often paralyzing fear and ability to cause great psychological or physical damage.

Of course, not everyone who was abused in childhood seeks out more abuse in adulthood. And not all people in abusive adult relationships were abused as children. But there is a correlation between what we are raised with and what we seek in adulthood. There is a connection between what is known and familiar, and what we—consciously or unconsciously replicate in adulthood.

For instance, it's likely that a gay man raised by a loving, patient, joyful mother who was consistently a healthy and positive role model would ultimately choose a relationship with a man he can count on, a man who embodies those same familiar qualities of love, patience, and joy.

We can hope that this kind of correlation between childhood and adulthood is, at least predominantly, a healthy and positive one, but it isn't always. This same man might not make such a rewarding choice, at least not right away. He might rebel for a while and seek out the perceived *opposite* of what he knows, for the sheer excitement of it. Perhaps he'll date impatient, moody, unpredictable guys. In this case, he's still acting just as powerfully on his unconscious motivations due to a significant relationship from his childhood, but in an alternate, in fact *opposite*, direction. You get the idea.

What most often happens is that we seek out many of the qualities of role models from our past, both the positive and negative ones, and some qualities we discover a fondness for along the way. We become our own person, greatly guided by the influential *known*, while we flavor and modify our desires with new discoveries about ourselves and others we encounter on our journey.

Bottom line, knowledge is power. Self-awareness can make all the difference between an enjoyable dating process and a destructive one. In my experience, teenagers and 20-somethings are not often the most self-aware people on the planet, and that's exactly the age when people are usually dating up a storm. It often amounts to a hit-or-miss, trial-and-error series of experiments, and we hope to have a good time and emerge relatively unscathed and more enlightened, although sometimes we become a bit more cautious because of the experience. If we're no worse for the wear, we move ahead, following our natural survival instinct, in search of a good match, a mate we feel will embody what we desire and require, coupled with that which is familiar.

• • •

As gay people we often have a dearth of *conscious* guidance and support from our families of origin regarding adulthood relationships in general and the fashioning of our gay love lives in particular. Therefore, I'm often asked for practical suggestions to help nurture all kinds of relationships, whether of the provisional dating sort or long-term commitments. During my years of clinical practice and writing advice columns for a variety of gay publications, I've developed some guidelines for increasing the chances of a relationship's success, especially during those formative dating periods. Even as our unconscious desires propel us into new situations, we can learn to adopt ways of becoming more successful at pursuing partnerships, friendships, and romances. So, without further ado, here are seven dating tips that have proven helpful to my clients.

SEVEN TIPS FOR DATING SUCCESS

Develop Your Communication Skills

Even when two people can forge a close understanding, a linguistic shorthand with each other, it's still important not to *assume* the other person knows what you mean. Assumptions lead to miscommunication and hurt feelings. If there's the slightest doubt, talk it out. At least half of the couples who come to my office need help developing their communication skills.

Remember, "It's Never About the Laundry"

A couple once came to me with the primary complaint that one partner always threw the clean laundry into the linen closet, while the other partner neatly folded and stacked everything. The neat one's *surface* complaint was about his partner's messiness. But underneath that feeling lay a sense of lack of respect and care, which, once the couple looked at it more closely, was revealed in *many* aspects of their relationship. The laundry was but one manifestation. The questions to address became: What was really going on here? And why did this carelessness—possibly masked hostility—exist in the relationship?

Know Thyself

As discussed earlier, maintaining a healthy relationship with another person begins by having a healthy relationship with yourself. Are you vigilantly honest with yourself? Only then can you be honest with someone else. Do you prioritize your self-esteem needs and take good care of your whole person—mind, spirit, and body? That's how you learn to be kind and take good care of another person. It requires commitment and attention. With practice, you can discover how to be your own healthy role model and therefore be the best partner you can be.

Communicate Your Feelings

Thinking is generally a more immediate process than feeling— i.e., you know what your thought is before you know how you feel about it. But communicating on a feeling level, while more challenging, adds depth, intimacy, and connectedness to your relationship. So before you blurt out something hurtful, take a deep breath, look inward, and identify the *feelings* you're having. It's a *head versus heart* thing. Chances are your partner is having some of the same feelings, and there you can find some common ground for honest discussion.

Fight Fairly

It's OK to argue occasionally. (In fact, heated discussions are one indication of passion.) A constructive argument can bring greater closeness when resolved, but a destructive argument can tear a relationship apart, if not now then in the future when your partner comes back for revenge, consciously or unconsciously. Here are a few pointers to assist the productivity of your arguments:

- Move the issue from *you versus me* to *you and me versus the problem*. It's a big shift in thinking, but it's an extremely valuable technique. If you're both on the same side facing the problem together, you begin to form a foundation of teamwork and trust, and you'll find that your partner isn't the enemy; the *issue* is what you need to address—together.

- Learn to be a patient listener. Before you state your opinions, pause to make sure you've really heard what was just said to you. If all your sentences begin with "I" or "my," you're not listening.

- Use a phrase such as "I feel" rather than "You make me feel…" It's less threatening and allows for nonaccusatory communication, while keeping the focus on feelings.

- Don't go to bed in a huff! The more familiar saying is, "Don't go to bed angry," but I don't think that's realistic.

If you're angry, you're angry, and if it's bedtime, guess what? You're going to bed angry. Staying up to fight will probably just make you more tired and confused. What's helpful is to acknowledge your feelings and commit to continue working together on the problem in the morning after you've rested a bit. An additional tip: Before you roll over, give your partner a kiss. It's a lot friendlier than a cold shoulder.

Develop a Support System With Someone Other Than Your Lover

To expect your partner to be your lover, mother, father, brother, sister, minister, teacher, healer, best friend, confidant, etc., is to set the relationship up for failure, set yourself up for disappointment, and set him or her up to feel resentful. Having other people of significance in your life helps you to keep a perspective, feel a sense of balance, and maintain healthy boundaries in your relationship.

Remember, You're Not Perfect Either

And who'd want perfection? Then there'd be no room (or desire) for a partner. We all want to know there's room for us in the relationship and that we contribute uniquely to our partner's quality of life. We all make mistakes, and we all deserve forgiveness. How forgiving are you of yourself—and therefore of other people? Remember the following 12-step adage: This too shall pass. Another personal favorite: Don't sweat the small stuff.

A Dating Meditation: "Learning From the Past"

We've all heard it from our friends and have probably said it ourselves upon occasion: "Oh, God, I hate dating!" Of course, some people really enjoy dating and do it well. In general, they find it to be a satisfying experience and revel in the newness, the excitement, the unknown, the early journey of the mating rituals. But, as many of you well know, there are plenty of stories about dating hell too.

And so, I'd like to offer you a helpful meditation for the trials and tribulations of dating. It's designed to help you begin to open some doorways toward enlightenment regarding your own personal issues of dating. Give it a try. You may love it.

For those of you who have read some of my earlier works, you know I'm an advocate of the meditative process for all sorts of internal growth, and that I myself meditate regularly. It's a wonderfully centering, enlightening experience, whether you sit *zazen* (a type of formal Buddhist meditation) or simply take a quieting breath to become still and experience some peace in the midst of a hectic day. Whether you spend an hour or a minute, if you are still and with yourself, you are in effect meditating.

Our conscious state has limits when it comes to self-understanding. Meditation helps us to unfold beyond those limits, to be more awake within ourselves and thereby live our lives more fully, with all the richness of and possibilities for growth, transformation, and healing. Meditation allows us to awaken our sense of ourselves, not only who we are but also what we are capable of. It helps us see the unfolding of our emotional lives one moment at a time. All of this and much more is possible when you incorporate meditation into your life. Even if you're a beginner, meditation will help you relax and see things more clearly. And the best part? All you need to do to begin is take a deep breath.

Remember: There's no right or wrong way to meditate. It's

an individual process. If you're interested in bringing meditation into your life as an ongoing part of your journey toward
self-awareness, there are many good books on the subject,
available in the self-help section of your neighborhood bookstore. There are several simple ways to enjoy the following
meditation: You can read it through, taking your time to pause
and absorb the ideas and questions; you can record it slowly in
your own voice and listen to it whenever you'd like; or you can
have a friend read it to you, someone you trust and in whose
presence you feel comfortable. That's my favorite way. You can
close your eyes and it's almost like having a friend give you a
soothing, relaxing massage for both the mind and body. So get
comfortable and let's start.

*Begin by taking several slow, relaxing breaths. Allow your
mind and body to begin to relax. Inhale and exhale. Take your
time. Again, inhale, and exhale. Let yourself relax fully.*

*Slowly and mindfully, feel the air moving into your lungs,
then feel the relaxation as you exhale. Feel your shoulders rise
and fall. Feel your chest rise and fall. Take in cool, clean air
every time you inhale, and breathe out stress each time you
exhale.*

Pause.

*Let your awareness come to your breath. Notice how your
breath happens all on its own. Witness how the body works
perfectly and in harmony, just as it needs to, all on its own.
Through no conscious effort of your own, the breath just happens. Notice it, be aware of it. Let it relax you body. Let it
relax your mind.*

Pause.

*Now let your mind begin to clear. Let it settle like dust par-
ticles falling to the ground. Picture your breath clearing out*

your thoughts. With each breath, the dust settles more and more. Relax. Settle.

Let your inner voice become quiet. Peaceful. Calm. Let yourself enjoy this feeling, this calmness.

Pause.

Now I invite you to go back in your mind to a time in your childhood. Flip through the pages of your personal history and think of your family, your friends, the adults who were important to you when you were young. Who comes to mind? Let the images arise and become clear. What moments, what places, what events are emerging? Take your time and make them real.

Pause.

How did you feel about these people? Why? How did you feel about yourself when you were with them? Why?

Pause.

Of the people who were significant in your youth, who comes to mind most often? What effect do you feel they had on you? What did you learn from them? What did they teach you that was positive or helpful? What did they teach you that was painful or disappointing? How are you feeling now, remembering this time?

Pause.

Take another deep breath. Which qualities from your past relationships are in your present relationships and friendships? Do you enjoy them? Are they hurtful to you? Are they in abundance? Are they scarce? Are they qualities you, yourself, possess?

Which of these qualities are you willing to nurture? Which are you willing to discard? How will you do that?

Pause.

You are a unique creation. You can become whoever you wish to be. You can love whomever you choose. You possess the ability to surround yourself with people who help you feel good about who you are. You can go to bed each night knowing you are loved.

You are loved.

Pause.

When you are ready, take a deep, centering breath.

CHAPTER
THREE

ON THE REBOUND: TRANSITIONAL LOVERS

*The trouble with some women is that they get all excited
about nothing—and then marry him.*
—Cher

One of the many grief groups I've facilitated over the years
consisted exclusively of gay men who had lost their significant
other. The loss was usually, although not in every case, due to
AIDS. In the early and mid 1990s, the face of AIDS was very
different from what it is now. And because the course of the
disease involved many variables, the course of death from the
disease was a study in variation.

Some surviving partners had been through a long illness
with their lover, and the ongoing emotional roller coaster had
taken its toll. When death finally arrived, there was a mix of
emotion that included, more often than not, relief. This sort
of reaction is completely natural, since part of the relief is felt
for the deceased lover who is no longer in pain, and part for
the survivor who can finally begin the long process of moving
on with life in whatever form it eventually takes.

Other group members had lost their partners quickly,
usually after a brief illness. At that time many people with

AIDS were beginning to experiment with non-Western medications and health routines and rituals entirely void of prescription medication. Their reasoning was in part based on wanting to avoid adverse drug interactions as well as long-term, potentially toxic side effects of taking certain medications. While homeopathic, metaphysical, and other forms of mind/body work are often a part of a person's wellness program today—whether or not he or she is HIV-positive—only a few years ago such methods were far more experimental. Patients who refused to take prescribed drugs sometimes fell ill, unfortunately, and died sooner than those who adhered to more mainstream treatment regimens.

Not everyone in the group had endured seeing a lover go through an AIDS-related death; heart disease and forms of cancer not related to HIV had claimed the partners of a few group members. But everyone had endured the death of a partner. This is an important point, because in some way all deaths are alike. The period preceding a lover's death is filled with emotional turmoil that may include anxiety, depression, fear, existential angst, anticipatory guilt, and concerns about one's own mortality. And there is the death itself, a trauma that takes many forms and manifests itself in ways as varied as the individuals involved, but is always on some level life-altering for the survivors. And there is a period of bereavement for the loved ones left behind following the death, the time during which survivors must wrestle with their loss and feelings of anger, abandonment, guilt, sorrow, relief, and depression. (For more about the stages of loss, see Chapter 15.)

In other ways, however, an AIDS-related death is *not* like other deaths and has very distinct characteristics—not only physical and medical but also social and political. For most of my adulthood I lived in Southern California, primarily in Los Angeles, where I did much of my work in HIV counseling and education and advocacy for gays and lesbians. Comparatively speaking, it's relatively easy to be gay in L.A. Much as in New York City or Miami, there's so much cultural diversity that people pretty much exhibit a degree of tolerance, if not acceptance, toward each other.

BIG CITIES AND SMALL TOWNS

In Los Angeles and nearby communities, lesbian and gay couples can be quite visible, especially in West Hollywood, Silver Lake, and other progressive areas. Many Angelenos have gay friends or acquaintances, and quite a few nongay people have lost a friend, acquaintance, or business associate to AIDS. This is not to say L.A. is a utopia. Racial tension, for example, has always been a problem, as in many big cities, and far too many instances of intolerance take the form of gay bashing or verbal, racial, or ethnic assaults. That notwithstanding, many gay folks successfully move to big cities in order to find a degree of acceptance, and in L.A. that's fairly easy to find. During the time I lived in L.A. as an out gay male working in the field of mental health, I rarely, if ever, encountered overt homophobia.

Following my 20-plus year stint in L.A., however, I lived for a short time in a Central California area near the Sierra Nevada mountains, a self-proclaimed Bible Belt where homophobia is alive and well and the social climate is totally different from that of the big city. In this part of California, homophobia covertly undergirds some of the region's politics and shows up more explicitly in conservative local media coverage of gay and lesbian issues as well as the lack of social services for sexual and ethnic minorities. But homophobia there can sometimes be quite overt, as in verbal assaults heard on the street. Perhaps it's all relative: North Carolina is where one of my friends hails from originally, and he has found Central California to be more progressive than where he'd come from. For me, coming from Los Angeles, Central California didn't feel progressive at all; living there made me realize the gay movement still has a very long way to go.

I offer these observations about provincial versus large metropolitan areas to illustrate an important aspect of grieving a loved one's AIDS-related death. When someone loses a partner to AIDS in less progressive parts of the country, the ways in which an AIDS death differs from other forms of death becomes all too apparent. True, regardless of where someone lives, decisions about treatment and insurance coverage usually favor blood relatives and/or heterosexual couples. But in more conservative communities, surviving loved ones are more likely to face a lack of empathy and understanding on the part of employers and the medical community. Family intolerance is often more common, and there can be a disturbing lack of general societal acceptance, acknowledgment, or practical and emotional help for the surviving partner. Therefore, having a good support network of friends becomes all the more important.

FILLING THE VOID

The grief group I facilitated was homogenous in that all of its members were gay males going through bereavement, and it was mixed in that everyone's story of grief was unique. A recurring theme among all the men, however, had to do with dating. Many of the men had been in long-term relationships with their lovers, and the internal void they now felt was palpable. These men generally attempted to fill that void in all sorts of ways, some healthier than others, whether through food, drink, drugs, gambling, sex, or work.

What the group discovered was that dating soon after losing a partner was often an attempt to fill a vast inner void where painful memories and loneliness lived. Dating wasn't so much about the unsuspecting new guy—who he was, what he was about, his interests, his personality—but about his ability to distract, to comfort, to soothe the surviving partner and maybe fill in for the partner who'd just died. Often, group members didn't even get to know their dates very well. After all, that wasn't the point, psychologically speaking. The point was to fill the emptiness and soothe the pain a bit. If a date could provide that, he passed the test.

Sex was often a big part of the equation. With sex a person can feel both distracted and soothed. And because it feels so good, some may begin to think this new date could be more than just the "rebound guy." He provides affection and fills an inner void; therefore, some may imagine, *I won't have to feel all this pain anymore. Maybe this relationship will take away the pain, and I can get on with my life again.*

True, some men actually do find true love following their loss, but more often what they find is true distraction. And there's absolutely nothing wrong with that as long as it's seen for what it is. Such relationships become problematic when the companionship and the physical intimacy of sex do not match the kind of connection that's truly needed. If the affair is just providing an emotional Band-Aid but neither person acknowledges that's the case, the eventual breakup becomes even more painful since, for the surviving partner, it carries the additional emotional weight of leftover grief for his dead lover. And, unfortunately, the transitional boyfriend is often thrown aside like so much flotsam, and that hurts both individuals. The

boyfriend may be left confused, hurt, and angry, and the grieving partner is left with having treated the boyfriend poorly.
This is hard on both men's self-esteem.

Of course, it doesn't have to be this way. I've known men
and women who developed good friendships with people who
in some way helped them through very difficult periods following a loss. The friendship, companionship, physical intimacy,
and/or emotional intimacy they were offered was truly of value
and very much appreciated. For them, no matter how things
turned out—a real love relationship or a nonsexual but endur-
ing friendship—they were able to receive help and feel the
closeness and warmth of another human being.

Here's a story I believe you'll appreciate and perhaps learn
from if you ever find yourself hurting with the emptiness and
loneliness that follows a significant loss. Given that no one is
an island or always a pillar of strength, this life offers many
opportunities to feel the pain of loss.

Dating up a Storm

When Mark broke up with his long-term partner, Terence,
he was, understandably, emotionally distraught. They'd been
together almost seven years and had hopes of being together
forever. Terence's alcohol and drug addictions made it
impossible, however, for Mark to stay in the relationship.
Mark had many reasons for wanting to break up, all of them
valid, although for many years he'd struggled with himself to
overlook them before finally deciding to call it quits with
Terence.

Shortly thereafter, Terence moved out of town, and the two
men fell out of touch with each other. What Mark began to feel
is common for people in his situation. I'll let him tell it in his
own words.

After the breakup, I felt as though a part of my guts had been ripped out. I had always heard about being left with a void when someone leaves you, but I didn't know that it could feel literally like an open wound.

We had an amicable parting of ways...we cried a lot. He was hurt, I was hurt. I had been angry a long time at him for his addiction, but then I didn't feel any anger, just pain, like my heart was breaking apart.

To make matters worse—or maybe better, depending on how you look at it—he moved away about a month later and didn't leave any information as to how I could reach him. So whatever ending we had was it.... There was no more I could do with him to finish business. It was over, he was gone, and I was alone. And it's funny, but even though it was my choice for us to break up, it still hurt like hell. I guess maybe it was worse for him because he was the one to get rejected, but it was pretty bad for me too. Just because it was my idea didn't mean I wouldn't feel all the pain and loneliness anyway.

Mark had come to my office for counseling during his second month of "dating up a storm." Shortly after our first meeting, we had the following conversation.

Mark: I was dating everyone. I probably averaged about five dates a week, usually going out with each guy once, sometimes twice. It was almost always sexual, but once in a while we'd just go to a movie or for some coffee and talk. The only reason some dates weren't sexual is when the other guy didn't want to [have sex]. When it was left up to me, I almost always brought the man home to my place or accepted an invitation to his.

Dr. Rick: What were you getting from all this dating?

Mark: That's hard to say. I think I got something different from everyone. Well, maybe that's not true, exactly. Everyone was different, but I got to feel some of the same comfort from their company. I got to feel some attention. It was a great distraction for me too. I got to take a break from feeling bad for myself and be the object of someone's sexual desire. Knowing that I was wanted, even for a night, went a long way toward helping me feel lovable.

Dr. Rick: Do you feel more lovable now?

Mark: [*laughs*] No, I don't, thank you very much.

Dr. Rick: Care to explain?

Mark: It's a temporary solution, very short-lived. For as long as the date lasted, and maybe even for part of the next day, I felt OK. It was distracting, having something—someone—to think about. The better the date, the longer I could get away from feeling bad about Terence. But it would last oh-so-briefly.

Dr. Rick: So that's why you needed so many dates per week.

Mark: [*after a long pause, with some tears*] Yes. Like a fix. I guess I'm more like Terence than I thought.

Several months later, Mark met a guy he started to date exclusively. The two men had not reached a verbal commitment to date only each other; Mark had made the choice to not see other men. I asked him about this new relationship.

Dr. Rick: So, how's it going with—?

Mark: Stew.

Dr. Rick: Stew.

Mark: It's going, I guess. Maybe it's standing still. I don't know, actually.

Dr. Rick: Standing still? How so?

Mark: I don't feel much. And I don't think the problem is with him. He's a great, very low-maintenance guy, but I hardly have any feelings about him. It's very confusing and unfamiliar.

Dr. Rick: Is it like you don't care for him as a person or for his company, or more that you don't have much feeling about him either way?

Mark: More like I don't have much feeling at all about him. It's like I'm shut down, which isn't like me. I'm hanging in there, though...like I'm trying to rationalize being with him, even though I'm not feeling much. Maybe I'm trying to legitimize this relationship purely by sticking with it—even though I don't know what I'm doing.

Dr. Rick: Well, you've been trying to avoid your feelings for a while now. All that "dating up a storm" in order to avoid the void, to distract yourself from the pain of your breakup.

Mark: Yes, so why am I not feeling anything now?

Dr. Rick: You're still keeping your feelings at bay. Not through the distraction of lots of guys, but through a shutting down, a numbness.

Mark: [*after a pause*] Stew deserves more than that. He's being fun and honest, and asks for nothing in return. He's noticed that I don't seem to offer much emotionally, and he did say something about it once. But I just laughed it off. So he's noticed. The guy deserves better.

Dr. Rick: Maybe you deserve better. Maybe you deserve to have your feelings.

During this discussion, Mark's therapy really began. It was the first time since his breakup that he began to allow his feelings to emerge. Until this time, he wasn't ready to feel the pain, so he avoided it. First he avoided it by distracting himself with dates. Then he gave that up and saw just one guy for whom he really didn't have any deep feelings—and avoided feeling pain by avoiding his feelings altogether. He began to shut down. And that's usually the way feelings work: You can't successfully select to deny certain feelings while allowing others to thrive, not for very long anyway. What really happens is this: *When you unconsciously suppress painful feelings, you suppress a certain level, a certain intensity, of feeling altogether.* So, if you avoid the lows, you're also avoiding the highs. If you shut down in an attempt to eliminate intense pain, you're also shutting out intense pleasure. Get it? What you're left with is a mild mid-range of emotions: very vanilla, nothing too tough but nothing too terrific either. The more you suppress, the more limited is your range of feeling. It's like living a beige life devoid of colors and interest, rather than a Technicolor life in which all the nuances, textures, and surprises are available to you.

It's a testament to Mark's conscious intentions that he was "hanging in there" and attempting to "legitimize" the relationship by staying with Stew. But what he came to realize is that Stew wasn't someone he wanted a relationship with—he was someone Mark was hoping to move on with. There's a difference. With increasing insight, Mark allowed more and more of his feelings to emerge and became able to see why he really wasn't being fair to Stew. It wasn't because he didn't feel anything; it was because he'd brought Stew into his life as a kind of prop, someone with whom he could experience companionship and mild feelings of comfort without being required—or being able—to offer anything back. Fortunately, both men were eventually able to communicate these issues and remain friends. As Mark says, they both will "keep the door open for when I'm *ready* to date...down the road sometime. After all, what's the rush?"

Sounds healthy to me.

~

I will take a breath and let my truth emerge.

~

I will be gentle with myself and with others.

~

I can survive this. I can survive just about anything.

Chapter
Four

A Work in Progress
(Or, When to Pick Out the China)

On the way to one's beloved, there are no hills.
—Kenyan proverb

You might know the following old joke: What does a lesbian bring on a second date? Answer: A U-Haul. Well, moving in together early in the dating process is not the sole property of lesbians. Gay men do it too. And you know what? So do heterosexual couples. Many couples move at the speed of light when feeling that first spark of excitement over the prospect of a new love. It's an exciting time: Fantasies abound, daydreams take over the workday, wistful grins are frequent, and a general lighthearted mood is the norm. This is a happy, hopeful, wishful time, and thoughts may naturally turn to wondering about the future and notions of spending a life together.

But hold on: It could be just a touch too soon to be browsing for housewares at Neiman Marcus. The rush of anticipation and the notion of a life together, while full of promise, can lead couples to hurry what would otherwise be a very enjoyable—and necessary—process. The dating period for you and a potential partner only happens at the beginning, and it's a period that can be looked back upon as joyous and fun-filled. It includes all sorts of exhilarating, nerve-wracking, titillating, sexual, emotional, and spiritual experiences. And it's a vital and important part of the process that brings two people together.

It's important to remember that, much as an individual grows, so does a relationship. It grows from one stage to the next, each subsequent stage providing the building blocks for the following. Early on, you and your partner may be in the "honeymoon period," that time marked by limerence (also called infatuation) and a certain light-headed feeling that keeps you soaring with exciting thoughts of your boyfriend or girlfriend. Limerence, though, is built on mystery, on the unknown, on seeing the other person *in*frequently. Therefore, limerence will decline over time as the two people spend more time together. (See Chapter 1 for more about this.)

Limerence does not, however, include clear, levelheaded, or practical thinking. Nor does it include even-keel emotional states. That's simply not what the feelings and thoughts are about during this time. This is not the optimal stage for making important, lasting decisions about the future of a relationship.

"Want to move in with me, Mary?" asks Kate. "Sure do!" says Mary. (And Mary's thinking, *She likes me that much! I finally found someone who likes me enough to ask!*) You're having great sex and discovering new qualities about her (and yourself, through her eyes) practically every second you're together. You daydream about her, everyday worries have fallen by the wayside, and life feels like a holiday. It's easy to be seduced into thinking this is what life will feel like all the time together. It's like vacationing in an exciting locale and being seduced into thinking that living there full-time will always be exotic and thrilling. "It's the real thing," says Mary to her friends. "It's love!" (Cue dramatic music.)

Well, it may *become* love. But at the very beginning, dear Mary, it ain't love, it's limerence. It's the very necessary foundation stage that precedes love. It sets the structure for greater, deeper feelings that may (or may not) come next. The problem occurs, however, when we attempt to fill an emotional void, a painful and ongoing loneliness, or an unresolved abandonment issue by jumping ahead in the dating process at a speed that denies any time for contemplation and self-awareness and rational thought.

Gay men and lesbians are the only people who have to fight to love. We fight in the courts, in schools, in churches, in our communities, and in our own families. Societal intolerance keeps us battling for what ought to be very naturally ours: the right to love whom we wish, how we wish. And to have that love acknowledged and validated. But social change is slow, and so when we find love, we want to hold on with all our might. The fear of losing it—after it was so hard to find in the first place!—is a mighty motivator. We may think, mistakenly, that moving in together is the way to cement the closeness, to somehow ensure its place in our lives, its longevity.

Meet Billy and James, who felt exactly that way.

Dr. Rick: So, how did you two meet?

Billy: At Apache [a Studio City, Calif., bar and dance club].

James: He was the most gorgeous guy in the place. I zoomed right in on him at about 10 o'clock. By midnight we were making out on the dance floor.

Dr. Rick: Sounds like a strong attraction.

Billy: It was for me too. I was so flattered when he came over to me. I had been watching him too—he just didn't know it.

Dr. Rick: So how did things proceed?

James: Quickly.

Billy: Way too quickly.

Dr. Rick: How so?

James: We moved in together within the first month. It was like three weeks, I think.

Billy: Yeah, I actually started moving some little things to his place during the first week, because I knew he was going to ask me.

Dr. Rick: How did you know?

Billy: I could just tell. He had that gushy look in his eyes and was totally falling for me. We were having a great time. I was falling for him too.

Dr. Rick: What made it such a great time?

James: The sex!

Billy: [*laughing*]Yeah, definitely the sex. We had sex constantly. I didn't know much about him then, but I knew every nuance of this man's body.

Dr. Rick: So you wanted to move in with each other because of the sex?

James: Actually, not just the sex. We really hit it off. We were having a great time like Billy says. And for me, I had never felt so close to someone so quickly. It was an amazing feeling, like this was the person I wanted to keep in my life. I knew how good this felt...I'd never felt it so strongly before, and it was like I wanted to keep this feeling going.

Dr. Rick: So you wanted to capture this feeling, keep it in your life.

James: Right. Like maybe forever.

Dr. Rick: And perhaps by asking Billy to move in with you, you could hold on to it forever.

James: Exactly.

Dr. Rick: Is that what happened?

Billy: No!

James: No.

Dr. Rick: What happened?

Billy: I wanted to move in with him just as badly as he wanted me to—definitely. But I had a nagging feeling about it. I was flattered and excited, so I went for it. I just thought we'd be able to overcome anything, because I really liked this guy. And we got along better than I ever had with anyone.

Dr. Rick: Well, you got along better in bed, anyway.

Billy: [*laughing*]Yeah.

Dr. Rick: And you ignored your "nagging feeling"?

Billy: Pretty much. It seemed minor. It was easy to ignore.

Dr. Rick: What about you, James...did you have any doubts?

James: I didn't have a nagging feeling, just a fear that I couldn't afford to let this guy go. I knew it was all happening fast, but that didn't matter at the time. I just didn't want to lose him.

Dr. Rick: And why was that?

James: [*beginning to cry*] Well, it took so long to find him. I looked my whole life for him. It felt like the most important thing in the world to hold on to him.

[*after a break*]

Dr. Rick: So you mentioned there were problems?

James: Yes.

Billy: Major problems. I felt like I had moved in with a stranger. We didn't get along at all—yelling, fighting.

James: We had constant arguments. And I heard myself saying things to him I had never said to anyone...mean things, like I was some awful out-of-control beast to him.

Billy: He was. It was awful.

Dr. Rick: How about you, Billy?

Billy: I was closing down. I yelled back over stupid things, like I had to defend myself over every little thing. Then I'd just shut up and not talk to him.

James: All the good feelings had gone. Just disappeared.

Dr. Rick: What feelings *were* you having?

James: I resented the hell out of him. I didn't want him in my space. I was angry all the time, but confused too. I didn't know what had happened. Was it me? Was it him? I was so depressed...I thought I had found real love. So, naturally, I started to wonder what it was I had felt. Do I even know how to love? Would I know love if it happened?

Billy: And I was very disappointed too. Very confused. I wanted to get out so I could clear my head. I believed he was a good person, but maybe I brought out his bad qualities or something. Maybe it just wasn't a good match. Good sex, but not a good match for the long run.

Dr. Rick: So what did you do then?

James: He moved out. We took a breather. I didn't want to date other people—I just needed a break to think.

Billy: I did date a few other guys, but I kept thinking about him, and then I began to miss him. So we talked on the phone, and eventually got back together.

Dr. Rick: But you didn't move in.

Billy: No!

James: [*laughing*] No, we just dated. We went much more slowly. We hadn't gotten to know each other yet, not really. We had been strangers living together and never had a chance to connect other than physically. I didn't know him.

Dr. Rick: So what did you find out?

Billy: That he's every bit the great guy I was hoping he was.

James: And I knew he was something special. We just didn't spend the time at the beginning to really find that out. I appreciate who he is now.

Dr. Rick: How are you feeling now?
James: I love him more than ever.

Clearly, James and Billy had rushed the natural process of dating; they were driven somewhat blindly by their excitement and hope, feelings that were largely based on a strong physical connection. Additionally, James had an intense fear of "losing something that felt so good," and Billy ignored his inner voice, one that may have wisely helped him make calmer, more rational decisions in the midst of a whirlwind of excitement. And while a physical connection is certainly an important part of the bond between two people and a wonderful way to express the closeness they feel for each other, it is only *part* of an ongoing bond. By rushing the relationship, they replaced their closeness with confusion, stress, and a great deal of disappointment. They moved in together, based on a *fantasy* of what they hoped the other to be, a fantasy that was fueled by some good times and great sex. James especially was filling a void, a void he had looked his "whole life" to fill. They didn't know each other; they just knew they each needed something.

These two men provide us with an excellent example of the danger of cutting short a period of courtship that could have included some of the hope and excitement they'd felt at the beginning. After honestly exploring their feelings and really enjoying getting to know each other, they could have begun to move forward. Fortunately, they eventually did the second time around. An important point: The suddenness with which their feelings ended when they first moved in together illustrates the irony of James's wanting to move in together in order to capture those very feelings.

Billy and James realized, fortunately, that they needed to

"take a breath." And this discovery came before they had caused their relationship any permanent damage. The breather provided them the luxury of getting to know each other in ways they had skipped earlier. And that provides us with an important lesson: The healthy route is to enjoy all the fun at the beginning and allow ourselves time to luxuriate in that phase, enjoying it, encouraging it to continue while other aspects of the relationship begin to unfold. It's the only time two people can feel all those feelings *for the first time together.* Why rush it?

So what is "too soon"? Well, no one can tell another couple exactly when it is too soon for them—that's one of those murky intangibles, unique to the individual and each couple. It's more felt than intellectualized *if* you are paying attention. And that is exactly the point. We can see from the above example the vital importance of listening and taking a moment to turn inward and identify what is really going on so you can identify what "too soon" may mean for you. If James had gotten in touch with the fears behind his impulses, he may have found ways to deal with those fears other than rushing into moving in with Billy. If Billy had listened to his sage inner voice, he may not have let a wash of flattery prematurely guide him into a situation for which he wasn't prepared. Being in the grip of romance can pose quite a challenge to this kind of thoughtfulness, this degree of self-awareness. And yet that is when it is most important. Remember: A relationship is a work in progress.

As a general guideline, let's say that "too soon" is when major decisions are being made before the couple has had a chance to build trust; when choices are based on loneliness and feelings of low self-worth, rather than the growing closeness and intimacy that can only happen with enough time spent learning about each other. Like an infant growing up through his or her toddler, childhood, and adolescent stages, a relationship needs nurturing, attention, and patience to grow healthy and strong. Circumventing the "wonder years" of a relationship by pushing it forward under anxious hope and the delusion of rapid and permanent closeness is like issuing a driver's license to a 4-year-old. It's too soon.

SEARCHING FOR WHOLENESS

One final thought: If we don't feel whole and complete as individuals, we may look to another person to complete us. In that urge to feel complete, we push and rush our relationships, confusing what we're ready for with what we think we want or perhaps need. It's akin to forcing a square peg into a round hole. As the saying goes, nature abhors a vacuum; it's human nature to want to fill the void within, so we attempt to do just that, with alcohol, drugs, overeating, compulsive behaviors of all kinds...and with relationships.

With another person, we may hope to feel the oneness, the wholeness we believe we lack. But this puts a tremendous amount of unconscious expectation on the other person to provide all that we can't be on our own. Without his or her consent, your new partner has unknowingly signed up to be the one to soothe your wounds and fill in your missing parts. So instead of just being able to complement each other and add pleasure to each other's life, there's an urgent, unspoken need imposed upon the relationship, adding tension, inevitable disappointment, and anger.

The solution: Take a breath. Look inward. It's in the attempt to discover ourselves that we form the real basis for any healthy relationship. We become vulnerable; we become aware—not for others but ourselves. It's fully up to you to pay attention; your growth is your own responsibility. Developing an ever-increasing capacity to love another, and to feel love returned, is a direct result of your commitment, first and foremost to yourself.

~

It is in the quiet that I discover myself.

~

In the quiet, I am in harmony with my universe.

~

I know who I am when I take the time to listen.

CHAPTER

FIVE

THE POWER OF A PARTNER

I'm like a book you have to read.
A book can't read itself to you. It doesn't even
know what it's about. I don't know what I'm about.
—Christopher Isherwood

An individual's self-esteem is intimately connected to the dynamics of that individual's significant relationships. In other words, your partner can—and does—influence your feelings of self-worth.

Pop psychology, personal growth workshops, and relationship seminars of earlier decades taught us that another person cannot "make" you feel a certain way. Only *you* can make you feel a certain way. Only *you* are in charge of your feelings.

Well, that's not entirely true.

Remember our discussion about vulnerability in the introduction to this book? When we allow ourselves to engage fully—emotionally, physically, and spiritually—and build an intimate life with another human being, we allow that person to have a great deal of influence on our perception of the world, our attitudes, our beliefs, and our feelings. We form with that other person a commitment born of the openness, desire, and love necessary for a healthy bond. As that bond is allowed to develop and deepen, it successfully does so through a reciprocal vulnerability. It's very much what being a couple is about. Yes, it is true that another person makes you feel a certain way, but *only with your permission.* OK, fine. However, do you think you are always in control of that process? And do you think you are always *conscious* of the permission you give others?

Think about a time when you fell head over heels in love. Imagine feeling that way now, right at this moment. Would you have the emotional strength to turn off that feeling? Do you think it works like a light switch with you at the controls, able to turn that feeling of being in love on and off at will? Of course not. And so we begin to see that another person, certainly someone who is important to you, absolutely has influence over how you feel. And it may be to such an extent that it doesn't seem you have any choice in the matter at all. It may seem, in fact, perfectly natural.

What has happened is that you have *unconsciously* given him or her permission, and that is a powerful ticket indeed.

If you trust another person enough to be vulnerable with him or her, then you are by definition endowing yourself with an openness, a receptivity. This openness lets the other person in, along with all of his or her thoughts, feelings, opinions and influence.We would like to think ourselves discerning enough to open or close those emotional gates to whatever degree we're comfortable, while remaining in control and shutting out any undesirable influence—but in reality that isn't how it works. That would imply that this process of letting someone else in is completely *conscious.* But it isn't. It is, in fact, largely a process of the *unconscious*, in which your feelings for another person may seem to take on a life of their own, your behavior follows suit, and the two of you become like a fabric that is woven together, sometimes loosely, sometimes firmly.

Here's another way to look at it: If you give your heart to another person, inevitably he or she holds a degree of power over your self-worth because, with vulnerability comes a certain lack of control. So, if your partner has an opinion about how you look in a certain outfit, it matters. If your partner wants to vacation in the mountains instead of the beach where you want to go, his or her preference can cause you some internal conflict. If your partner has had a bad day at work and comes home in a dark and oppressive mood, the climate in the house—and in your personal emotional universe—changes. If you're attuned to your partner, if you're emotionally intimate with your partner, some degree of inner conflict is unavoidable.

If your partner finds you fascinating and hangs on to your every word, your self-esteem as reflected in your partner's eyes soars. You absorb many positive feelings about yourself because of the quality of his or her attentions. It feels good. Even better, *you feel good about who you are:* the person your partner sees while enraptured with you.

Likewise, if your partner's attentions subtly yet unmistakably convey that you are of no particular worth to him or her and you are not held in high esteem, then you absorb that message, which results in damage to your sense of self-worth. If you have formed an emotional bond with your partner, if you care about what he or she thinks and says, then you are affected—in this case, negatively.

A brief story about a former client comes to mind. When Sheila first met Lori several years ago, she was happy and excited to be entering a new relationship, but in a short time something began to nag at her. She was aware that Lori had a subtle but unmistakable tendency toward criticism. Lori would pick at her about the little things that she did differently from the way Lori was used to from her previous relationships. This dynamic increased considerably after they moved in together. Lori's criticism began to take a toll on Sheila, who had always thought of herself as a competent, responsible person. In time, Sheila's self-esteem began to suffer, and she started to think of herself as someone who couldn't do anything right. The more Sheila allowed Lori's criticism to sink in, the more she began to think that everything she attempted fell just short of the mark. She cared deeply for Lori, but she also cared what Lori thought and said about her. A reducing, discouraging, frightening dynamic had settled into their relationship, and Sheila felt resentful over the toll Lori's criticisms were taking on her self-image.

Their bond, like any other, required that Sheila be open (and therefore, vulnerable) to Lori's impressions of her and take in her thoughts, feelings, and perceptions just as Lori took in Sheila's. Unfortunately, what Sheila also absorbed was an ongoing, insidious criticism that eroded her self-worth. It's a high price to pay and a good example of how being emotionally and psychologically open to another is *not* purely a conscious decision. If it were an entirely conscious process, Sheila would not have allowed herself to be the vulnerable recipient of ego-bruising messages from her partner. Instead, she could have let in what was loving and closed the door on what was not. A relationship with this kind of dynamic will either end because of the pressure one partner imposes on the other, or will evolve through greater acceptance to allow for each person's differences.

Sheila's situation is such a powerful argument for the

importance of choosing to surround yourself with people who are loving, accepting, and validating of who you are! And so we begin to see how important it is to seek relationships in which you are encouraged to thrive, where you feel the support and admiration that allows you to blossom into becoming all you are able to become. Like a child, a relationship is an organic entity; it lives and breathes and grows, born of the unique energy and attention given by its parents. If it receives loving attention from both partners, it grows into a healthy entity. If it does not, it suffers. Such is the power of a partner.

It is important to remember that part of the privilege—and responsibility—of being in a love relationship is understanding the issues that comprise a person's psychological and emotional strengths and weaknesses—one's own and those of the significant other. I asked several couples who are all in relationships that have lasted at least five years what they thought were the most important dynamics within a relationship. As a starting point for discussion, they came up with the following as being particularly influential on each other's self-esteem: **anger and arguments, communication, humor, commitment, and closeness.**

Specifically, I asked—sometimes interviewing one partner, sometimes both—how these qualities play out in their relationships. I wanted to find out not only how they handle problems and what has gone into forming their long-term bond, but also which issues are most *important* to them as partners, particularly in terms of self-esteem. These are couples with whom I have worked professionally—as colleagues or clients—and some are friends and acquaintances. These concepts were just a starting point for discussion. I invited these couples to discuss anything they felt was important to their relationship, and offer any advice that might help other couples. Here are their frank comments, along with some of mine.

ANGER AND ARGUMENTS

First, let's look at how some couples deal with **anger.** Anger is a tricky one. (Where would we therapists be without it?) No one I know has ever been taught how to effectively deal with their anger, because anyone in a position of teaching them was uncomfortable with their *own* anger. It may just be the most uncomfortable and challenging feeling there is for many of us. And yet, tackling both the *feelings* of anger as well as the *expressions* of anger can help enormously with understanding the interpersonal dynamics of a relationship.

> When Jon and I first met, we said terrible and hurtful things to each other during our arguments. It felt more important to win the fight than to settle the issue at hand. We'd yell a lot, and our words definitely cut into each other's self-esteem. We didn't know how to resolve problems back then, so our arguments were very unproductive and unhealthy for both of us. Now when we have a fight, we go to separate corners for five or 10 minutes and take deep breaths. This calms us down and keeps us from saying anything hurtful. Then we usually hug, go into the living room, and remind ourselves that we love each other. We try and think about what the real issue is, and we just start talking. We may still be angry, but at least we're not taking it out on each other, saying nasty things that hurt and can never be taken back. Our arguments are much more productive now, and we don't cut each other down. The key is that we've learned to

remember that we indeed love each other; we don't want the other guy to feel bad about himself just because of a difference of opinion.

These men have worked hard at learning how to argue more effectively—and lovingly!—and arrived at a healthy solution for themselves. Rather than let an argument escalate into a hurtful yelling match where nothing productive is accomplished while they take damaging shots at each other's self-worth, they take a breath and calm down so that they can *talk*. This is a great way to create a space in which you can work a problem through to its conclusion. They're not attempting to deny themselves their feelings; they're simply achieving maturity in how to *express* those feelings. The following couple provides another healthy example. Lovers for 14 years, they have learned through a painful process what works for them, and what doesn't, when it comes to arguing.

One thing we learned the hard way is that when we'd have problems or arguments, we used to each go and tell our separate friends. It was how we unloaded and de-stressed, gained some sympathy, felt vindicated, had a shoulder to cry on, etc. Then we realized that when we'd go back to each other, we'd act like nothing's wrong. In actuality, the problem was still there, we'd complained about it to others, and we'd made no progress whatsoever as a couple. In fact, it started to deteriorate our relationship. It put a distance between us, like we each had this smug superiority over the other. I felt vindicated by my friends, and she did by hers. So, over the years we've realized that talking to outsiders at the exclusion of each other really doesn't work. We need to first and foremost talk with each other and try our best to work through the problem. If we can't do it alone, *then* we go to others—together— for help.

Sometimes couples get into the habit of communicating with their friends *about* their partners, instead of communicating *with* their partners. This is different from casual conversation; it is a way to experience what therapists call "secondary benefit," meaning, it's a way to get your cookies, your strokes, and in this case some sympathy. In the retelling of the problem to others, you get to talk about it, you get to come out looking good—the brave one, the victim, the survivor— and your partner comes out as the villain. What does this accomplish? Increasingly poor communication at home and, over time, resentment between both of you. Further, it gives a message to your partner that you don't trust your ability as a couple to work through your difficulties together. So now you've got a trust issue on your hands. The solution: Talk with each other. I sometimes tell couples, "When all else fails, try communication!"

Sally and I never fight. Never. We eat, we drink, we bake, we go for long drives, we flirt with other girls... anything but fight. Our sex life sucks. My self-esteem is at an all-time low.

These gals never learned to fight fair. (See the section in Chapter 2 on fair fighting.) So they avoid it altogether for whatever their individual reasons—reasons that may be understandable, undoubtedly acquired from past experience but nevertheless unhealthy.

People generally avoid confrontation for one or more of the following reasons:

- They are afraid of their own feelings, others' feelings, and what might happen when these feelings are unleashed.

- When their childhood role models (parents, grandparents, or other authority figures) fought, it was frightening, anxiety-producing, destructive, messy, or hurtful.

- They are prone to feeling guilty, so they would rather hold it all in than be the cause of hurting someone else, thereby having to experience the resultant guilt, shame, or embarrassment.

- They tend to bottle up their feelings; they're so afraid that if the dam cracks even a little, it will be a destructive, irreparable explosion. (And it might well be, especially if they have held in their feelings for a long time.)

Also, remember that fighting is a sign of passion. It is passion released in an angry form, but passion nonetheless. So of course this couple's sex life would be suffering. If there's no passion emotionally (in this case, anger), there's likely no passion sexually. And if anger is absent, then there's also no real joy, excitement, happiness, or any of the feelings that we usually enjoy experiencing. Getting in touch with why they don't fight would be a good first step toward repairing their bond. Therapy is very helpful toward that end.

I like how Tim and I communicate our anger. We don't rant and rave...usually! Instead we try to just talk about it. Our discussion might get a little heated, but we don't turn nasty toward one another. We used to let issues build up, until we were filled with resentment, then took it out on the other guy and didn't even deal with whatever the real issues were in the first place. After all these years, we've learned better. It's not about keeping silent, but it's not about hurting the other one either. It's just about expressing yourself and listening to him express himself, then doing our best to solve the situation one problem at a time.

You go, boys! These men were in the same support group as the two men in the first example. Again, this couple, too, has discovered the difference between having feelings and expressing feelings; between a constructive argument and a destructive one. They keep in mind that they love each other. They've also learned not to let their issues—and feelings!—stew, piling up one upon the other until they're ready to explode. Anger is a feeling. It needn't be a weapon with which to hurt someone you profess to love.

COMMUNICATION

Good communication is truly the foundation of all successful relationships. While some folks are blessed with the innate ability to communicate clearly and succinctly, for others who struggle with their communication skills, take heart: Good communication is learnable. It requires understanding, some healthy examples, and it takes practice. Let's start here.

I think our communication needs a lot of work. Anytime Frank and I talk about something we disagree on, we sort of shut down. It's like the conversation comes to a standstill and we run out of energy to go on. Or like we're afraid to upset the other guy with something we might say. Or maybe we don't want there to be too many areas where we disagree because that will mean we're incompatible, and neither of us wants to find that out. So we stop talking before it's too late.

• • •

It's remarkable how little Jill and I can discuss. There are only so many topics that feel safe, and there are, it seems, lots of topics that don't. It's getting worse as time goes on. We're approaching our sixth anniversary, and we hardly talk anymore. It makes me feel very insecure in the relationship.

Frank and Jill and their respective partners prove that good communication doesn't necessarily just happen, no matter how long a couple has been together. It takes commitment and conscientious effort. Good communication comes naturally to some people; for others, it is an acquired skill. However easy good communication is for a couple, it provides the cornerstone of a healthy relationship that cannot be taken for granted. In the first example, the couple mentions several possible reasons that are excellent starting points for exploring in therapy what the real issues are. It becomes a real relationship problem when two people can't discuss what's on their minds. It's the big white elephant in the middle of the room. In the second example, we see the toll poor communication takes on the quality of the relationship: feelings of insecurity and doubt.

Roger and I are doing OK in the communication department. In fact, a lot of times we feel as though we can complete each others' sentences. I think we're very close, and that shows through our communication. We talk about whatever we want to, and we know that the other man will listen. We don't talk a lot, but when we do, we feel heard. In fact, just thinking now about what a good listener he is makes me smile.

Roger and his partner seem to be in a healthy, comfortable place regarding their communication. What a wonderful feeling to experience really being *heard*. Who was the last person who really heard you? How did that feel to you? What kind of a listener are *you*? Do you hear just the facts? Do you also hear feelings? Are you waiting for a break in the conversation so you can speak, rather than really listening to the other person? There's a saying that the opposite of listening isn't talking—it's *waiting*.

HUMOR

One thing gay people have been adept at is creating a sense of humor as a way to fit in, as a defense against the nonacceptance of others, and as a way to get through what can be a difficult life filled with challenges that others, unless they are familiar with what it means to be an oppressed sexual minority, cannot fathom. Some uses of humor are wonderful and healthy; others are not. Lifting oneself up at the expense of others is an example of an unhealthy use of humor. So is using humor to avoid discussing the real issues, such as in a relationship where communication is already problematic. Irony, nonhurtful sarcasm, and humor that does not rely on the belittling of others, are examples of healthy humor.

Oh my gosh, if we didn't laugh, we'd cry—or kill each other. This is what I love about my relationship: When

Josie and I are fighting, there almost always comes a time when someone says something ironic or ridiculous and we just crack up. We don't then avoid the confrontation that still needs to happen, but we proceed a bit more lighthearted than previously, and we recall how much we really love each other, even in the midst of an argument. But even more, we just like to laugh…not only during a fight, but we have a true talent—mostly Josie!—for seeing the absurdity of life and spending part of every day having a good laugh. It's one of the ways we are bonded together, and one of the ways we can feel good about ourselves: that we have this talent for laughter.

• • •

Humor has saved our relationship. Bruce and I laugh best when times are tough, and I thank God for that. I guess we just get overwhelmed sometimes, and when we hit that point we just bust up. Once one of us is laughing, the other guy starts laughing too. After a good laugh we seem better able to deal with whatever life is throwing our way at the time. It's great. It's very central to who we are.

• • •

William says that I don't have a very good sense of humor, but I don't agree with that. His humor is often in the form of put-downs. He denigrates others because he doesn't feel good about himself. Hello, Psych. 101? He's a very insecure person, and his family raised him to have many self-doubts. So his humor isn't what I consider funny. I think I'm more of a look-at-life's-irony kind of person. Put-downs aren't funny to me, but the absurdity of life surely is. We're working on the roots of William's humor in therapy, and I think we're making progress. When it's aimed at me is when we have difficulty as a couple. It really angers me. There's a big difference between laughing with your partner and laughing at your partner.

The bond between couples is varying and personal. Whenever you wonder what in the world your best friend sees in his or her "awful" partner, remember that there is no real way you can understand fully the bond which exists between them. It's between *them*. Whatever has attracted one person to another, and whatever then holds them together and creates a closeness that they alone share, may not even be on a conscious level. But it is most definitely felt on a gut level and guides the course of their relationship. Humor is one of those qualities that has the ability to bring two seemingly very different people together. It is also considered to be a sign of intellectual and emotional compatibility: being able to laugh together—such a wonderful and powerful tool for bridging differences and feeling close when it's used in a healthy way.

COMMITMENT AND CLOSENESS

Commitment and closeness are grouped together in this section because as two individuals get to know each other over time, their emotional commitment to each other naturally strengthens. The more emotionally committed they become as a couple, the closer they feel and the stronger their bond. They experience a deepening of feelings. Self-esteem increases. Their attraction to each other goes far beyond skin-deep. It's a healthy cycle. As one client simply put it, "I love having someone to love.

> When I first laid eyes on Jeff, I knew I was in love. I know lots of people say that, but my strong reaction to him was not based solely on looks. There was a kind of energy about him, a peaceful, quiet, strong energy that was immediately evident to me. As we dated, my feelings were proven to be more and more true and accurate. I picked up on it right away, and even today I could not be more in love with him. He makes my day constantly in a million little ways. He has a big effect on me. I've never felt this close to anyone before, not even my parents.

• • •

> When I was single, it seemed that all the guys I ran into were not interested in a commitment of any kind. Well, I guess they were committed for that night, but that's it. It really took a toll on my self-esteem, because I was feeling that the only thing I had to offer someone was good for one night. Then I met Gary, who was as into commitment as I was. What a relief! He was cute, smart, funny, and into commitment! We're celebrating our tenth anniversary next month.

• • •

> Susan and I never thought we'd become a couple. We worked together and were great coworkers. I always found her attractive, but didn't think she was available

emotionally. I didn't see any way someone could really get close to her. But I'd always found her attractive physically. So one day I thought, *What the heck, I'll ask her out.* As I got to know her, I realized that there's so much more to her than what I could see at the office. She was warm, open, and came across as brutally honest about her life and her emotions. What a wonderful surprise to discover that getting close to her would become the journey I'd hoped for my whole life. Now it's like a special bond between us that I know her so well, and almost no one else does. We've been together a long time now. She may be hard to get to know in public, but in our relationship we're very, very bonded. It's a gift that makes me feel so fortunate to know her.

• • •

We have a lot in common, Buddy and I, and we love, laugh, work, play, have great friends, share three dogs, travel together, and grouse about our parents. That's our bond. Couldn't ask for a better one.

I hope these examples have helped you to understand and appreciate the power of a partner, both the good and the bad. While different people want different forms of an ongoing commitment, it behooves us to realize there are certain qualities that are essential to any healthy relationship, whether it's with your lover, a member of your family of origin, or one of your friends. Perhaps you were able to identify with some of the issues the couples in the preceding examples have been grappling with; perhaps you can learn from what works for them (and what doesn't) and draw out some wisdom to apply to your own relationships. After all, your quality of life and your self-esteem as well as that of your significant other are the important things.

One of the messages I hope you received from the comments and stories illustrated in this chapter is that a successful relationship requires commitment. It takes both parties committing to the ongoing process that is the living relationship. Emotional health, personal growth, and unimagined happiness are all available just under the surface of whatever relationship difficulties may be at hand. And if both of you are committed to the process, then you can take heart that there is always hope. Always.

~

I am committed to helping my partner feel good about himself or herself.

~

I allow my self-esteem to grow with the help of my partner's love.

~

A healthy relationship is no accident.

Chapter Six

LONG-TERM RELATIONSHIPS: WHAT WORKS AND WHAT DOESN'T

*Until one is committed, there is hesitancy, the chance
to draw back, always ineffectiveness.*
—W. H. Murray

More and more lesbians and gay men are showing their desire for long-term monogamous relationships. Perhaps one reason is the growing awareness of the possible consequences of having multiple partners for casual sex. The loss of so many people to AIDS brings to the fore the need for some relationship permanence and stability, a desire to have someone you can count on, someone who will not abandon you. More people are realizing not only that there is physical safety and comfort in being in a long-term relationship, but also that having the level of love and commitment that is part of going the distance is like having a built-in security blanket. And that means being able to count on someone who loves you deeply just for who you are. For increasing numbers of gay men and lesbians, this represents a great deal of security.

Others are finding that creatively designing their own non-monogamous versions of long-term companionship is right for them and provides the kind of life they desire. Whether a couple is monogamous or open, being embraced within the arms of a loving, ongoing, committed relationship with a partner/soul mate/spouse adds quality and texture and richness to one's life. It increases happiness and a sense of "belongingness," and therefore has become an important—and deserved!—goal of many gay men and lesbians.

In the gay and lesbian community, one can find life partners who have been together 20, 30, even 40 years. This is nothing short of remarkable, when one considers the emotional trials and tribulations throughout history as well as the *physical* dangers inherent in being gay or lesbian just a generation or two ago. Then of course, for the past 20-plus years there's been the challenge of trying to find love in the midst of the AIDS pandemic—as if it isn't already hard enough to find a partner with whom one feels compatible!

While gay life was significantly harder in many ways for earlier generations—not that it's always a hayride these days—many long-term couples have overcome tremendous adversity and provided a life for each other filled with commitment, respect, and love. How did they do it? In many ways they are our relationship role models, these forefathers and foremothers. Whom did they turn to for guidance regarding long-term relationship success and, even more important, what advice might they pass along to us today?

More recent generations have disregarded the social stigma of seeking counseling and therapy for help with personal issues and therefore realize the value of receiving professional help for relationship difficulties as well. How about these present-day role models—what have they learned to ensure their long-term success? And what advice might they offer us about maintaining the level of intimacy and commitment required for spending a life together—for 20, 30, or 40 years into the future? Even with the great strides the gay movement has made worldwide, life often isn't easy for many of us—far from it, in fact—and long-term gay relationships still face many unique challenges. How, then, can gay people today grow into successful, committed relationships?

To answer this question, it is important for gay people to look to solid role models. I am a firm believer in learning from our gay brothers and sisters, both our contemporaries as well as our ancestors: their histories and struggles, their wisdom and guidance. We can learn from everyone we know, whether they are single or involved, young or old, regardless of ethnic background, religion, or personality. We learn what works, as well as what doesn't, by paying attention to others.

Society has improved significantly from what previous gay and lesbian generations experienced—especially in urban areas, but in increasing numbers of small towns as well. Still, when it comes to relationship difficulties, there are some tried-and-true solutions that many couples, both past and present, have found tremendously valuable. In the following excerpted conversation, a lesbian couple shares how they've applied some of these solutions to difficulties they've encountered. Certainly, they've experienced their ups and downs as a couple, but through their commitment to each other they've found ways to learn and grow together. I have summarized some of their comments, but much of the following reflects their exact words. Meet Donna and Stacy.

HOLDING CLOSE WITH OPEN ARMS

Dr. Rick: You've been together for a little over 10 years now, and you still seem very much in love. How did it all begin?

Donna: Well, we started as friends. We were in school together, which gave us a wonderful opportunity to learn some important things about each other. Things like how each of us deals with stress, our senses of humor, our creativity and stamina in working toward goals, etc. We forged a real friendship based on this common goal [completing grad school], and that created trust and knowledge of each other, which has turned out to be our foundation as a couple.

Dr. Rick: What do you think is valuable about couples who start out as friends, as opposed to starting out some other way, such as being sexual partners.

Stacy: I believe that—at least in our case, and from other friends we've heard this same thing—if you aren't friends underneath it all, you can't have a successful long-term relationship. It's perhaps the foundation that gives you the confidence and sets up the trust that enables you to be a couple in the first place. It's also true that if you don't *really* adore each other as well, it'll be hard to weather whatever life throws at you and survive as lovers. The one thing that is certain is that the circumstances of your lives together will change, and each of you will change. The question is whether your love for each other is generous enough to allow that to happen.

Dr. Rick: So, given your foundation of friendship, how are you able to weather life's difficulties as a couple?

Donna: I've found out that in order to be happy together, I must take responsibility for my own happiness and try to contribute to Stacy's and vice versa. This is different than taking responsibility for each other's happiness. We have been in the most trouble over the years when one of us is feeling, for instance, depressed over an extended period of time, and doesn't take care of it herself and doesn't feel the participation of a helping partner in the process. This devastates both parties.

Dr. Rick: Do you have an example?

Donna: A few years ago I was completely depressed about my job, and I kept trying to hang in there and see if it would improve. Meanwhile, I spent hours ranting and raving to Stacy about how terrible it was, how angry and trapped I felt. She was, of course, not in control of my situation and at her wit's end watching me suffer. Our sex life and our general intimacy suffered. We really drifted apart during this period because I wasn't taking care of my own business. When I finally did, not only did my personal happiness soar, but our relationship improved. I have to hand it to Stacy for hanging in there when many of her needs weren't getting met. This, to me, is true love.

Dr. Rick: What's been the fallout from that period? Did you return to status quo? Grow closer for the experience? Did feelings heal?

Donna: It would be incorrect to say that our relationship totally rebounded—it didn't. My being depressed and remote for so long has changed forever how we relate to each other. Stacy was sad and mad for a very long time about it, and it changed what she expected from me and what she felt she could give me. That has been hard for both of us, but we both accept that was what grew out of the situation. We can live with it.

Dr. Rick: What about those *external* stressors that you mentioned earlier? You talked about circumstances of life changing and about each of you changing as time goes on.

Stacy: I really think that sometimes externals shift in such a way that a couple can find themselves in major crises. An example from our lives is when we were in a position to consider becoming foster parents for my little niece, who was in an abusive home. This happened almost overnight. We agreed [to become foster parents] in order to keep her from having to go live with strangers for a year or more, but we had no period of adjustment—it happened that quickly. So everything in our lives changed. It was a joint decision to take care of this young girl whom we loved, but the adjustments were immensely difficult for several months at the beginning. We had to figure out who was in charge of which parenting duties, and we had to change Donna's home office into a bedroom. My niece now needed to attend a new school, and there were family support issues and a lengthy and stressful process in the courts. The stress of all this pulled us apart in certain ways, but also brought us closer. We got to see each other in parenting roles, and we learned how to make good, healthy decisions for a child in need. So even though the stress was hard, it was also incredible to find ourselves communicating constantly and lovingly, and we learned to relate to each other in ways we never would have without the experience.

Dr. Rick: So you each grew from what life threw your way.

Donna: Absolutely!

Dr. Rick: What would you say is the most prominent difficulty facing long-term relationships?

Stacy: Probably a chief difficulty in long-term commitments lies in what we are told about them societally. We are told that either they cannot work, or that you must find the one special princess with whom you will be madly in love forever. Our reality is somewhere in between and is probably different for each couple. I think successful relationships rely heavily on shared values, good communication, and good chemistry. There's probably some luck and fate thrown in the mix too.

Dr. Rick: Speaking of chemistry, how's your sex life after 10 years?

Donna: Our sex life is not as hot as it was the first few years, but we still enjoy regular sex. It is important to us, and we would both strongly prefer not to be in a sexless long-term marriage. We try to make time for it. And when we don't have sex for a while we miss it and want to reconnect as soon as possible. We each think the other is the most beautiful woman in the world. We can still take each other's breath away!

Dr. Rick: Sounds wonderful. What's been the most important resource to you as a couple?

Donna: We're blessed to have strong community support—Stacy's family and a network of both gay and straight friends. We've had surprisingly few major glitches in our relationship, and when we have, we've used therapists and the shoulders of good friends to help us through. Although we had a rocky transition from friendship to lovers at the beginning, it ended up being useful. We found out so much about each other at that time—fears, desires, goals, limitations—that we didn't have the sometimes unpleasant surprises that come with learning about that stuff after you've committed to each other. I think it's tremendously disillusioning to be hot for someone and then, after the honeymoon's over, realize you don't really know them at all or that you're really different in ways that are important to you. Doing it the way we did has assured much more stability, I think.

Dr. Rick: Do you have a "relationship philosophy"?

Stacy: Neither of us can imagine being truly happy without the other. But if one or the other of us needed her freedom, it would happen, although it would be gut-wrenching. e.e. cummings said something in a poem about "holding close with open arms." I think that sums up what Donna and I try to do with each other.

Donna and Stacy provide us with a great example of a long-term couple who work well together because they both value the health of their relationship, no matter what challenges may arise for them. Their priority is clear: Their relationship is the most important part of life to them, and as changes occur, external as well as internal, they willingly and intelligently enter a process of finding the resources they need, communicating, supporting each other, and learning from their mistakes. Perhaps one of the most important aspects of their relationship is that they are both on the same page, philosophically. They feel mutually the wonder and love of being together and are motivated to take responsibility for themselves as individuals and do whatever it takes to ensure their love and happiness as a couple.

~

I am committed to honoring the needs of my partner as well as my own.

~

This is the relationship I have chosen; it is mine to nurture.

~

This is my life...right here, right now.

CHAPTER
SEVEN

THE OPEN RELATIONSHIP

Don't you know what your 20s are for?
They're for having sex with all the wrong people.
—Bette Midler

I am a fan of monogamy.

There, I've said it. I believe that when two individuals fully dedicate their sexual, emotional, and spiritual energy to the growth of their relationship, the bond that forms between them is among the most powerful—and intimately satisfying!—that a couple can achieve. That said, monogamy isn't necessarily for everyone. Nature/God/Our Creator makes everyone unique. So why should we think that monogamy is the ideal against which we all must be held, like some sort of relationship standard that is supposed to fit everyone the exact same way? (Such thinking is only a few degrees away from the belief that says everyone should be heterosexual!) Just because I believe in monogamy doesn't mean everyone else does. However, this book is a collection of the techniques I have found to be healthy and helpful, and they have all been filtered through the lens of my own life and work. So, you're stuck with my conclusions. But as I tell my patients, do your best to absorb all new ideas and feelings that may help you on your journey; the rest you can set aside for a later time. One never knows when the teacher will be allowed entrance by the pupil.

Speaking of "shoulds," when I was completing my undergraduate studies, I had a wonderful human sexuality teacher who was very supportive of people finding their own truths. She strongly advocated that everyone needs to explore his or her sexuality, regardless of professed sexual identity. In fact, she once disclosed that she wished she were bisexual: "I feel I'm missing out on half the fun!" she quipped. Cool gal. Regarding "shoulds" she said, "When it comes to your feelings, don't 'should' on yourself and don't 'should' on anyone else either!" I always try to remember that advice.

A Tricky Situation

Now, let's face it: Open relationships can be tricky (no pun intended). As a therapist, I've worked with a lot of couples over the years. For every couple I've been acquainted with who has an open relationship and seems to be genuinely happy about the arrangement, there are probably 10 couples who aren't at all happy about their situation. Or at least one partner isn't. Have they just not worked through the problem spots yet? Are they just following the example of so many gay couples who have open or semi-open relationships and doing what they think they "should"?

This isn't to say that open relationships can't work; obviously, for some people, they work very well. But I don't often come across couples for whom opening up their relationship would be a healthy idea, no matter what their difficulties together may be. In fact, many gay couples who have come to my office are struggling with the consequences of one partner straying from the monogamous relationship they had at one time believed they both desired and agreed upon. The problem may relate to a one-night stand, an ongoing affair, or a burgeoning shift in what is wanted by one partner but not the other. Whatever the particulars, the underlying issue is now about trust—and abandonment, betrayal, hurt, anger, and resentment. The spectrum of underlying emotions can get complicated and tricky—as well as challenging and painful.

Also, many lesbians and gay men delude themselves into thinking that an open relationship is just fine with them. Their thinking goes something like this: *It's an open-minded approach—everyone's doing it. I can handle it with no problem, or at least can grow to be OK with it in time. Besides, it may even save my relationship!* Well, that sounds like a lot of rationalizing to me.

As lesbians and gay men, we are all too accustomed to accepting second best in a myriad of ways because that is, by and large, how society conditions us to think. Take, for example, the difficulty we are currently experiencing nationwide in our attempts to attain the same human rights as heterosexuals: the 1,000-plus legal, financial, and societal benefits that accompany a legally binding marriage. Because of our conditioning from a very young age, we are sometimes inclined accept a relationship arrangement that, while not ideal, is at least *something.* Unfortunately, this means we're accepting the morsels instead of the meal. It means accepting a family invitation to the reunion but not being able to bring your partner. It means not having the final say in your mate's health care. It means not being able to adopt in all states. It assuredly is not taking care of yourself and your needs. You get the idea.

Such an unhealthy and powerful set of negative messages

begins at the highest levels of society and trickles down through local governments, schools, churches, and communities. It's an insidious toxic message about being second-class citizens that affects every aspect of being gay: employment, housing, legal rights, medical decisions, and of course, relationship choices. If we feel we're second-class, we'll accept second-class. Until, of course, we consciously become aware (and outraged) enough to make a change. If you're in a relationship in which you are increasingly and consistently unhappy, perhaps it's because you've settled for a situation you feel you deserve. You may not want it, but you believe you don't *deserve* better. This is what you've been taught. This is the message you've internalized.

BEING HONEST WITH YOURSELF

The question becomes: Are you just kidding yourself due to societal messages that you've internalized, settling for second best and denying your true needs, or are you being honest, self-aware, and defending your sense of healthy self-esteem? This is one situation where "just say no" may actually be valid.

I've worked with many couples in which one partner or the other, when they get to an honest and insightful place, realizes that he is not really happy with having an open relationship. However, he loves the person he's with and isn't willing to give up the "good qualities of the relationship" just because his partner wants to have sex with other men. In couples who have been together for a number of years, one person sometimes becomes restless with the sameness of it. Instead of entering therapy to look at what's going on underneath the restlessness, they open the relationship in a misguided attempt to cure the problem. Obviously, this can be quite a painful situation for the partner who doesn't want an open relationship.

Some couples who initially agree to bring others into their bedroom, may simply open the door for jealousies and hurt feelings. Sure, they've made a conscious decision together, but they have created a rift in their bond that may or may not be repairable. To avoid such a problem, some couples adopt a "don't ask, don't tell" policy and see other people on the side but don't talk about it with their partner. The situation can feel a bit like having a big elephant in the middle of the room: Everyone knows it's there, but no one's talking about it. And once there's an agreement—verbalized or simply "understood"—*not* to talk about certain issues central to a relationship, it becomes easier and easier to add to the list of topics that are taboo. Thus a precedent is created whereby communication degenerates, suspicion increases, and the bond erodes.

On the other hand, some couples do indeed find a way to create new rules for themselves whereby an open relationship is mutually agreed upon and ironically becomes a way for the couple to remain together. They find that it's the right solution for their needs, and while other sexual partners are part of their life together, they enjoy the security of coming home to each other and the love they have remains intact. While some couples successfully evolve into such an arrangement, this seems to work best in relationships when each partner, while single, was specifically seeking someone who was also looking for an open relationship. It takes a very specific type of bond between two people—and a degree of rigorous honesty free of self-deception and rationalizations—to be able to maintain a strong and undamaged sense of emotional intimacy while partaking of physical intimacy outside the relationship.

Here are two open relationships illustrating some of the issues that are representative of what many such couples go through.

Meet Pete, 47, and Josh, 32, a couple who've been together for more than 12 years. They concur that their relationship was exciting and satisfying for the first few years. Then, something happened that caused a lot of stress between them for much of the next decade. This, briefly, is their story:

Pete: When Josh and I met, I wasn't expecting a relationship. I was in what I call my playful mode, and wanted to have some fun for a while—you know, meet some cute, compatible guys for physical fun—no strings, no commitments. But that didn't last long. I was in a local bar having a few drinks and I saw Josh. He had good looks, but something else too. I couldn't quite put my finger on it. So I went over to him and we started talking. Sure enough, he turned out to be intelligent, funny, thoughtful, unassuming, and it all made him sexy as hell to me.

We started dating and things moved along pretty quickly, although I must say that the pace felt quite comfortable to me. The sex was great and we got along really well. We were growing closer and closer, so after a few months we became exclusive, and after about a year we decided to move in together. I figured I was done with my playful phase and had gotten that out of my system.

The problems really occurred, though, shortly after, when I started to feel a bit closed in and restless. Josh wasn't doing anything wrong—it was me. Never having lived with anyone before, I felt suffocated. I lost interest in having sex together and decided I wanted to open things up a bit, thinking that would help. My hope was that I would somehow gain a renewed interest in the relationship and in having sex with Josh.

Josh: Everything was going along fine, until Pete wanted to open up the relationship. First, he wanted us to invite other men into our bed so we'd be playing with others together. He suggested that there wouldn't be any jealousy that way. That was not the case at all. To make a long story short, Pete enjoyed himself, but it didn't work for me. I was *extremely* jealous! And worse, I felt very unloved whenever we'd have a third guy with us.

So then, he decided he wanted to see other men "now and then," but not bring them back home nor tell me about it. He figured that that way, I wouldn't be jealous because it wouldn't interfere with *my* life, or our life as a couple. Again: wrong! This made me jealous all the time because I never knew if or when he was with someone else. He could be playing around on his lunch hour or after work before I'd get home— anytime. And of course, his not telling me if he was [playing around] or not just made my mind work overtime, so I wondered constantly about where he was and what he was doing and with whom. Every time we were out and he'd spot a guy he found attractive, I'd wonder if he was going to pursue sex with that guy. It was crazy-making! And, it did a number on my self-esteem because during this whole time I kept wondering why I wasn't enough for him.

Pete and Josh have spent the majority of their relationship with this kind of tension between them. Sometimes it lessened, as Pete would declare he'd had enough of playing around and just wanted to settle in again with Josh and be monogamous ("Usually after some bad sex encounter," Josh claims). Josh would, of course, be less anxious during these periods and feel closer to Pete. But after a while—a period of time that would vary over the years—Pete would desire sex with other guys again, and the cycle would start up all over.

Josh feels that this cycle, although anxiety-producing, is a price he's willing to pay to have Pete in his life. He'll tell you that he's profoundly unhappy with the situation but claims to this day that he is very much in love with Pete and grateful to have someone like him in his life.

Pete states that he is indeed in love with Josh, but he'll tell you he's found it's simply in his nature to desire sex with others from time to time, or else he'll feel very trapped in the relationship and end up bitter and resentful of his partner.

Let's look a little more closely at what's going on here. As these men talk, it's clear that Pete has a tone of remorse about hurting his lover, and Josh speaks with tremendous frustration and a kind of helpless outrage. This situation, while long-standing, is not working out for these guys.

If Pete had suggested they seek couples counseling instead of having three-ways or seeing other men secretly, they would have been better able to express to each other all the feelings they have about the changes happening between them. Even though Pete sometimes feels "trapped" and uninterested in sex with his partner, his experience is not so uncommon, especially for someone in a long-term relationship. Since Pete had never been in such a relationship before, he doesn't realize how common his feeling of being trapped is, nor would he know what solutions might work better than opening up his relationship with Josh. Couples counseling, if they had started it earlier, could have suggested some options and set them on a healthier therapeutic path. Undoubtedly, they would have uncovered issues, thoughts, and feelings of which neither were fully aware, and therapy would have helped them come up with tools to deal with their difficulties *together*. They would have worked as a team to make any necessary improvements or changes in the relationship, instead of one partner causing the other great hurt and frustration. This cycle of trust and betrayal has hurt their relationship. It's an unnecessary and unsatisfying way to spend a life together.

• • •

Earlier I talked about couples in which each partner sought out the other based on a mutual desire to have an open relationship. Sam and Max are a good example of such a couple. Here they share their thoughts on their relationship:

Sam: I'd been in a couple of relationships before, and what I've realized is that I'm just not cut out for monogamy. And believe me, I tried. I have a deep capacity to love my partner, take care of him, spend wonderful time together in and out of bed. But I need more sexual adventure than I can get from just one person. Even experimentation with my lover isn't quite the ticket. I need to play with totally other people, who bring a different style of lovemaking, a different body type, a different personality into the picture for me. Some of my friends consider this selfish. I don't. I just know what I need. I have a strong sex drive and a strong appetite for a variety of sexual experiences.

I was very clear about not wanting to be with someone with whom this would have to be a secret of mine. I wanted a lifelong partner who felt as I did about this issue. So when Max and I started dating, this was one of the first things we talked about.

Max: I totally get where Sam is coming from, because I feel the same way . I do *not* want to be restricted to one person sexually, and I do *not* want to lie about it. I wouldn't do that to someone I care about. Maybe down the road we'll get tired of playing with others. But for now, this arrangement is good for us. We still sleep together every night, we have great sex, and we get along like best buddies. He really is my best friend, in part because we see eye to eye on this very issue. We've been together almost four years now, so we're doing well with this arrangement.

Sam: I want to add that I love Max very, very much. In fact, this is the best relationship I've ever been in. It's certainly the most honest and direct. So I feel confident that if anything was bothering Max about us each seeing other men, he'd tell me. And I would tell him if it bothered me. We'd work something out, I'm sure. I wouldn't consciously do anything to hurt my lover.

Max: We go to all sorts of bear events, and usually those end up being very sexual times. Lots of couples are there doing what we're doing. And everyone is pretty up front about it. And if they don't want to play with a guy who's already involved, that's cool. At these events sometimes Sam and I play together with others, and sometimes we each go off on our own. We come back and tell the other what's going on, so that's how we keep our trust in each other. That's the most important thing for us: trust. I love Sam more than anything. I won't do anything to violate our bond.

Do you believe Sam and Max are being honest with each other and themselves? One can't always know if another person is sitting with their truth or their denial, but these guys seem very straightforward to me. If one or the other begins to have doubts or problems with their open arrangement, I believe they will speak up and take steps to work through the issues. Are they happier with an open relationship than they would be with a monogamous one? They believe they are, and they've been together for several years. Their relationship started out as open, and both men continue to want that kind of understanding in a partner.

These points are genuine: Sam and Max have an ongoing relationship that they each want very much to continue; they are emotionally committed to each other as both friends and lovers; they love each other and do not want to cause hurt; and they prioritize their communication and a willingness to work through any difficulties that may arise. These are important qualities for any healthy, long-lasting love relationship. For this stage of their lives together, they've found something that works quite well for them.

If you're contemplating whether an open relationship is right for you, I'd like you to consider the following guidelines. Several of my colleagues and clients have shared with me over the years what has helped them maintain a strong bond in the face of nonmonogamy. In their various relationships they have created rules to live and love by. These represent a short set of mutually agreed-upon *dos* and *don'ts* that have allowed trust to continue and grow between them. The following is a synthesized collection of these guidelines, one that will hopefully serve as a starting point for your own thoughts about the issue and as a way to open dialogue between you and a partner if the two of you are considering such an arrangement.

FIVE TIPS FOR A SUCCESSFUL OPEN RELATIONSHIP

"Don't Ask, Don't Tell" Doesn't Work

Either partner reserves the right to ask any questions and has the right to expect honest and clear answers when he does. Communicate your hurts, resentments, or jealousies immediately. Ignoring them or letting them fester unaddressed contributes to an emotional shutdown and a desire to retaliate.

Whatever Specific Rules You Decide Upon Must Be Honored

For instance, if you agree not to bring anyone home to your shared bed, be sure to uphold and never violate that agreement. If you promise not to let outside play interfere with your time together, make sure that's a value you both share and are willing to abide by. If you both agree to your mutually created guidelines, you will better abide by them.

Many Open Couples Agree to Play With Others Together and Only Together

This allows them to share in the excitement of newness *as a couple* while still retaining their bond and sense of commitment to each other. It may, for some, be an opportunity to create ongoing sexual friendships. Some couples choose to play with any new person (or couple) only once, to avoid emotional entanglements outside of the relationship. If problems do arise, however, be sure to communicate feelings at the first opportunity.

Be Tactful and Considerate

If you've ceased having sex as a couple but want to have sex outside the relationship with others, be sensitive to the feelings of your partner at home. Do you both enjoy sharing with each other the excitements and titillations of the affair, or do you *not* care to hear about all the intimate details? Such a situation provides readily available opportunities to express anger in a passive-aggressive manner. I encourage you to look at your situation honestly, and to evaluate the impact—and the feelings involved—of having sex with others while not having sex with your lover.

Always Play Safely

The last thing you want to do is bring health issues—from easily treated medical problems to HIV—into your partnership at home. Many people seek sex outside of their relationship to fulfill their differing sexual tastes. Maybe someone else is wilder than your lover, and this is something you seek. But wild or mild, vanilla or kink: use protection!

Perhaps most important to remember is that relationships, like any living things, need to be well cared for, nourished, and cherished. A significant relationship is an emotional investment—an investment in your own happiness and the happiness of someone you care about. Soul mates don't come around too often. One can never waste love, patience, devotion, or care on another person, especially someone with whom you trust your heart. If you are self-aware enough, careful enough, and ready enough to meet and develop a relationship with someone you are prepared to love, handling it honestly, lovingly, and with generous care may be the best investment you ever make.

~

A healthy relationship is within my power. It is up to me.

~

I am committed to being honest—first with myself, and always with my partner.

~

My process is ongoing, unique, and valid. It is mine.

CHAPTER

EIGHT

THE EX: FRIEND OR FOE?

Those whom we love we can hate; to others
we are indifferent.
—Henry David Thoreau

Pretty much every dating adult, gay or straight, has a "significant ex." At *least* one. Not everyone, however, has an ex-partner who is a good friend, a trusted confidant, or someone who continues to be a valued member of his or her "family." In fact, some people are not in touch with any of their exes and have never experienced any degree of civil communication after a breakup. They consider themselves fortunate if the ending was minimally acrimonious. Once it's over, it's over. Time to move on, right?

Well, let's look more closely at the issues involved. The transition from lover to friend can be difficult. Not all relationships end on a positive note, with the love and mutual respect necessary to maintain any sort of follow-up friendship. And certainly there are situations, as in the case of a physically or emotionally abusive relationship, in which it is neither desirable nor healthy to maintain contact with the abusive partner, at least not until enough time and counseling has occurred for healing to take place. And even then, caution is advised.

But when a love relationship ends, there's often a great deal of good to salvage and transform into a rewarding future friendship, if both people have the tools—and desire—to do so. Hearts and minds have come together when a person has spent a significant period of time in love with a partner—making plans, making love, and sharing some of the most meaningful aspects of life together, whether they lived together or not, whether the relationship lasted months or years. We're talking about an intimate involvement in which some of the most precious parts of who you are have been woven together with those same parts of another person, creating the fabric of a love relationship. Whatever the reason for the breakup, perhaps there are still aspects of this relationship, this emotional investment, that can continue to enrich the lives of both individuals for many years. In other words, just because the status of "significant other" has come to an end, that doesn't necessarily mean that a transition into "friend" is unattainable. To simply assume it is may mean missing out on a wonderful opportunity.

In fact, the love-relationship void—left somewhere in the middle of your gut, no doubt—may in time be filled with a friend-relationship that could prove to be even more rewarding than what the two of you used to have together. As mentioned earlier, just because a couple stops being a couple of lovers doesn't necessarily mean they can't be a couple of friends. With a healthy dose of self-awareness and an honest look at the relationship issues involved, it is entirely possible.

The Friendship Test

There are times, of course, when maintaining a friendly relationship after the breakup of a love affair is just impossible. But what if a good friendship can be created? Wouldn't you hate to look back later and realize that the reason you are short one good friend is because you didn't give it a try? That in your moment of hurt—or anger, resentment, or confusion—you simply didn't allow for the opportunity of a transition? You weren't receptive to it, so it didn't happen. Maybe you were too upset; maybe you shut down. Perhaps not enough time had passed to heal the hurt. Perhaps having a friendship with this person was the last thing on your mind.

OK, fair enough. But now that the dust has cleared and a bit of time has set in, here's your opportunity to be open to the possibilities. The following are questions I would encourage you to ask yourself in an effort to learn from the relationship, while discerning the potential for salvaging a friendship. I recommend that you do this exercise alone and really give yourself time with each question and reflect on the answers that arise. And remember: These questions can be applied to any past or estranged relationship—with lovers, family members, former colleagues, acquaintances, or friends.

- How much anger am I feeling about the relationship?
- How much guilt do I feel about the relationship?
- What first attracted me to him or her?
- Which of his or her qualities do I like the best?
- How many of those qualities are still available to me?
- What, for me, are his or her least-desirable qualities?
- How many of those qualities would likely remain in a friendship?
- What, more than anything else, characterized our bond?
- What would characterize a friendship with this person?
- Am I able to forgive him or her?
- Am I able to forgive myself?
- Why would I like to keep this person in my life?

Give yourself permission to be completely honest. After meditating on these questions, whether you now are pursuing the renaissance of a friendship or not, what's truly important is that you'll have examined the nature of your thoughts and feelings regarding this person, instead of participating in a careless severing marked by a lack of introspection and self-awareness. You may find that your answers lead to more questions about yourself. Perhaps one of the obstacles you face has to do with your own (lack of) ability to forgive. Perhaps you're facing some realities about your emotional availability and your potential for love and commitment. Do you suppose you are to blame and are therefore beating yourself up while feeling too ashamed to take more positive action?

An important point to mention here: There's a big difference between taking responsibility and berating yourself endlessly. Taking responsibility, when it is appropriate to do so, is an act of maturity. Self-berating is self-destructive, a product of low self-esteem, and keeps an individual in a "woe is me" cycle that *avoids* the taking of responsibility.

So take your time. Ponder. You don't have to decide right at this moment. This is an opportunity for you to examine the issues. Personal growth happens as it needs to and as you are ready for it, so long as you are open to exploration and growth. The answers to the above questions can give you valuable insight into your own personality, the dynamics of the relationship, and a sense of your ability to invest emotionally in a new type of friendship with your ex.

Let's be clear about something: I don't mean to imply that any of us should decide entirely with our heads—and not our hearts—who our friends are. In fact, the way we choose our lovers and our friends is *not* based on logic at all! Relationships are based on the heart, on desire, on our unique set of conscious and unconscious needs. And our needs spring from our specific personal histories: the kind of upbringing we had and what we were taught to value in another human being; who our formative role models were; whether the parenting we received would later encourage us to choose partners who could enrich our already "whole" selves—grounded in a sufficiently intact sense of self-worth—or partners to whom we would look for completion so we could fill in emotional gaps and soothe early life wounds. The psychological landscape of a person's history directly influences the choices he or she makes every day; choices that may be insignificant or life-altering, deeply personal or merely practical.

Perhaps the whole point of having had past relationships is to learn from them. What better way to feel a sense of accomplishment and growth than to be assured that, even though it didn't "work out," it was all worth it. Remember this: The lessons are as available to you as you are willing to make them. The end of a relationship is a rich opportunity for acquiring the kind of self-awareness that informs your future relationships and allows for new learning that can repair previous wounds and help make up for any deficiencies from your childhood.

Remember that one of the beauties of a good friendship, as opposed to a romantic or sexual involvement, is the lack of expectation and accompanying tension. It seems that we are far more able to accept a friend for who she or he is, flaws and all, than we are a lover. And, when working toward the transition from lover to friend, that degree of acceptance could be a relationship's saving grace.

The following real-life story illustrates one couple's journey from lovers to becoming best friends and is an excellent example of the kind of care, consideration, and respect required for making such a healthy transition.

BREAKIN' UP IS HARD TO DO

When it became apparent that Robert and William had reached a point in their relationship where they both felt they could go no further with each other emotionally, it was, in their words, "the hardest day of our lives."

"Remember that old song," asked Robert, " 'Breakin' Up Is Hard to Do?' What an understatement!" William and he still felt a great deal of love for each other, and they cared about each other very much, but for the past six months they had felt their romantic connection had reached its end, and was like, in William's words, "a rubber band that has been stretched for all its worth but can do no more."

One of the signs they both noticed that proved to be indicative of their nearing an end was that they had stopped looking toward a future together. While they used to dream of someday buying a house together and had many conversations about which neighborhoods they liked, now those dreams had somehow run out of steam. They weren't so much fantasizing about building a future since they were just "putting in our time." They felt they were existing instead of growing, stagnating instead of moving ahead together. After five years as a monogamous, loving, devoted couple, a quiet giving up had occurred. This is much different than when a couple has settled into a comfortable routine after their dreams have been realized and they're able to enjoy the results of their efforts together. For Robert and William, their situation had a feeling of loss—as if something they had once hoped for was no longer going to happen. And more to the point, neither of them much wanted it to happen.

After the first couple of years, their sex lives had diminished somewhat, a fairly common and natural occurrence. That wasn't the part that concerned them, though, since they still had a regular and rewarding sex life. It was this sense of loss, of giving up, of losing steam with the relationship that brought them to seek counseling. During therapy they realized they were both feeling this way; they just hadn't articulated these thoughts and feelings to each other previously. And it was confusing: How can a couple still love each other yet feel that the "life partner" or "significant other" aspect of their relationship has reached its end? Wouldn't most couples love to have what they had? Wouldn't other couples like them simply stay together and open up the relationship by taking outside boyfriends for a little spicing up, but still remain together as a couple?

Perhaps that's how some other couples might handle their feelings, but it wasn't the solution Robert and William were seeking. Staying together in an open relationship while no longer wanting to remain life partners didn't fit with the level of commitment they valued toward each other. And to what purpose would they "open up" the relationship? It wasn't their sex lives they were concerned about. It was their thoughts and feelings about each other, specifically about their future as a couple, that were shifting. If a transition needed to be made, taking outside boyfriends wasn't the transition they wanted.

And so, after making a very painful decision, they broke up. Their friends and families were understandably concerned and provided much empathy and support. And perhaps more importantly, Robert and William provided emotional support *for each other*. In therapy, they talked about how it all *felt*, this ending. It wasn't always easy: At various times guilt and/or anger were prominent as well as a strong sense of failure, some regrets, and much more. And whenever one of them wanted to talk about it, the other was right there, ready to listen, hold, comfort, and listen some more. They held each other in high esteem and realized that no matter how supportive their circle of friends were, they found that they themselves provided the most-needed salve for this very painful time. They entered a period of mourning for the relationship they would no longer have, for the dreams that had now ended, and found that they provided each other with the best bereavement group they could ask for. They mourned together and kept communication open and honest.

This realization led to others: that they had *always* supported each other emotionally, that they were good listeners, that they had each other's best interests in mind, and that aside from love, they also felt a genuine *like* for each other. As William says, "We were protective in a brotherly way, made each other laugh in a best-friend way, and cared about each other as if we'd grown up together." Clearly, there was much to salvage here.

Add the fact that the two of them had traveled together extensively and loved to do so. They shared many interests, especially movies and books, and genuinely enjoyed spending time together. It became clear that while they may not have desired their "lover" status to continue, they made excellent travel buddies and wanted to continue to see movies together and share good books. They were rediscovering the best parts of each other, those parts they wanted to savor. And learning this helped their grieving process enormously. Where before they had experienced a lack of hope for their future, they were now looking forward to a future as good and dear friends who know each other well and share a variety of interests. They wasted no time in planning a short trip together, to sort of "test the waters" of their new friendship. And while this transition certainly didn't happen overnight, they were excited about a renaissance of their relationship, one where they set each other free romantically while providing a secure friendship, a safe haven, a type of "home" where they could always return for emotional well-being and comfort.

When asked about the single most important aspect of their successful transition, they agreed that it was the unconditional, nonjudgmental support they were able to offer each other. "If you love someone all those years," says Robert, "you don't suddenly stop caring for him. You may be hurt. You may be angry, but ultimately, after you work through all that, you want what's best for him. Some form of love survives."

William concurs: "We're even better at the friendship thing than we were at the lover thing. All those years of caring allowed for a friendship to grow, no matter what else would happen to us. For that, I will always be grateful."

Robert and William provide us a love story with a very happy ending: a successful transition from partners to best friends. And while they may certainly encounter bumps in the road—perhaps a degree of jealousy when one of them starts dating, maybe recurring feelings of acute grief over the loss of being together as a couple, undoubtedly various other opportunities for introspection and self-awareness—they have formed a foundation that will help them through any rough spots. They have a valuable friendship, a commitment to the well-being of each other and a pattern of support they can cherish for the rest of their lives. They will always know that they matter to each other and that their love has survived the formidable test of change.

KEEPING THE BEST PARTS

As mentioned earlier, partners do not always desire to remain friends after a breakup—and certainly for less obvious reasons than overt physical abuse. Emotional abuse can be subtle, insidious, and just as destructive—even more so—in the long run. There are times when it is far healthier for your self-esteem not to keep an ex in your life. If you feel worse about yourself when you're around your partner, if you become unhappy just thinking about having to go home to him or her, or if you can remember consistently feeling better about yourself *before* this person entered your life, then something destructive is happening to your sense of self-worth, likely as a direct result of this relationship. Once you muster the courage to address these issues head-on, the result may well be that you want to be free of this destructiveness. Therapy is an excellent way to sort through these issues.

Another common reason to choose not to remain friends is if at the start of the relationship there was no basis of friendship on which to build a foundation of trust, care, and other roots of longevity. Then, feelings ranging from apathy to outright acrimony would negate any desire to make the transition to friends. And this is perfectly valid. How many people have had relationships that were based on seeing the other person through rose-colored glasses because the sex was great? Or perhaps you've had a relationship that was based on some short-lived need that just wasn't fulfilling enough to sustain for a longer time? Or maybe, after the first few encounters, you just didn't like the guy. Fair enough.

Meet John and Paul, two gay men in their 30s. Their real-life story illustrates some of their difficulties and also provides a helpful example of a healthy way to keep the best parts of an unhealthy relationship after it's over.

John and Paul lived together in John's house for about two years and had been dating for a year prior to cohabiting. But shortly after Paul moved in, they began to have problems. As

John tells it, "Paul's true colors came out right after we set up house together. It was like he was charming and romantically persistent while we were dating, then, once he got what he wanted [moving in], he became unbearable."

Paul turned out to be abusive to John in ways both subtle and obvious. He wasn't just passive-aggressive; he kept putting John down verbally and was destructive in the way he carelessly broke John's things and caused damage to the house. Further, Paul's previously undisclosed health issues placed John unexpectedly in a care-provider role, a role Paul took advantage of by staying unemployed and not contributing to household expenses. It was a bad situation that continued to get worse: Trust was violated, tension was increasing, and any care or attention given to the relationship was growing ever more one-sided. John has a kind heart and wanted to give the relationship every chance to improve, but eventually he realized that it was beyond repair. Understandably, he felt he had been conned and taken advantage of in many ways. And he wanted to play the victim role no more.

After their breakup, they remained housemates for a period of time to give Paul a chance to find a new place to live. This, as you might imagine, did not work out well either: The abusive partner simply became the abusive roommate, attempting to sabotage John's efforts at dating other men and continuing to take financial advantage of the situation. John had no way of knowing the depth of Paul's psychopathology—he is not a psychological professional, nor was he aware that Paul's particular personality type excels at "the con"—and with no small dose of selfishness. But what John did understand was that his kindness and generosity was being abused, his self-esteem was suffering in the process, and this living situation had to end.

Throughout these trials and tribulations, the one aspect of

this relationship that John consistently enjoyed was the friendship he developed with two of Paul's relatives: his sister and mother. During family visits, John would gladly entertain them by showing them the sights around town. Paul's mother shared her recipes with John, who loved to cook, and the sister shared John's passion for photography. They all celebrated several holidays and birthdays together, and it felt to John that, despite the obvious problems in maintaining any sort of friendship with Paul, the relationships he had developed with Paul's mother and sister were well worth keeping, so he committed to nurturing them.

Long after Paul moved out, John has been able to continue warm and mutually enjoyable relationships with Paul's mother and sister. He did not turn his back on the whole situation, which he could have done once Paul moved out. Although communication between John and Paul has remained minimal, the laughter and camaraderie John shares with Paul's family members continue to provide a level of satisfaction he deeply values. John's efforts to work toward a closeness with them, despite the wounds left over from the relationship he had with Paul, have resulted in rich rewards for being able to salvage the best parts from this challenging chapter of his life.

In applying the lessons from this story to your own breakup, it's worth thinking about what you're willing to give up and what you wish to keep. Often, when a couple "divorces," peripheral friendships are also lost. If those who entered your life as a direct result of your union were really "his friends," then you may simply accept that they too will now exit from your life. And perhaps it is with a degree of stubborn pride, some hurt feelings, or embarrassment—or because of simple carelessness—that once-treasured friendships held in esteem are jettisoned unnecessarily. This question is well worth considering: Although it takes both parties to commit to making a friendship succeed, where are you with your part of that effort? How willing are you to toss aside valued friends because of a love relationship gone sour? Perhaps that is when you will need those friends most.

Remember, happiness is not an expendable luxury. Good friendships mustn't be treated as expendable either.

~

To the best of my ability, I will move forward with forgiveness and awaken to learning—wherever that journey may lead.

CHAPTER

NINE

TENDING YOUR HEART

I always wanted to be somebody.
Now I realize I should have been more specific.
—Lily Tomlin

Books about relationships tend to be fairly behavioral, with tips, bits of advice, and guidelines to follow for success. And this book does indeed offer some of that. Practical suggestions can be helpful, but behavior alone isn't what's really at the core of successful relationships. So let's close the first section of this book by looking at what's beyond behavior, especially when it comes to significant relationships.

A successful relationship begins with the self. Read that sentence again. Internalize it. Perhaps write it on a piece of paper and tape it to your bathroom mirror—it's a keeper. A successful relationship with anyone else starts with knowing yourself, understanding your wants and needs, and being patient and understanding with the work in progress that is you. And a healthy relationship with yourself requires not only insight but also a vigilance about self-honesty.

Knowing yourself—having insight into what makes you tick—must include being as honest as humanly possible with yourself. What is more important than being true and honest with yourself about your needs and your interpersonal talents and strengths as well as your limitations? How else are you to get to know who you really are? This is easier said than done, of course, because many of us have a remarkable talent for telling ourselves what we want to hear and believing what is convenient to believe. We sustain thought patterns that fit our image of who we want to be and who we *believe* ourselves to be. We practice selective listening and selective vision, especially when it comes to our self-images and ideals. We hold tightly to those ideals we have relied upon. It is a survival technique, this selective perception, and we've had our entire lives to perfect it. We do it well.

But is it an honest portrayal? Maybe yes, maybe no. How we see ourselves often is partially true and partially not true. Depending on our level of insight and commitment to self-awareness, we experience varying degrees of understanding who we are, and who we are *in relationship* to others.

And this has much to do with our level of self-care. How well do we take care of ourselves, not just physically, but psychologically, emotionally and spiritually? Who are the people we surround ourselves with, and are they *care-full* of the relationship? Do your friends, lovers, and family have your best interest at heart with all they say and do? Do you feel that you matter greatly in their lives? Do they matter greatly in yours?

SELF-CARE

One of my favorite self-care images—it's a reminder, really—is a physiological fact that's taught to medical students during their training: The first task of the heart is to pump blood to itself.

When I give talks to care providers, counselors, mental health volunteers, families, and those working in HIV-related fields, I discuss something called "healthy selfishness." The concept usually raises the eyebrows of those who hear it for the first time; so conditioned are they to think of anything associated with the word *selfish* as negative. Yet, healthy selfishness has become a concept that has grown tremendously in importance, not only for people caring for others but also as a widely accepted philosophy for healthy living.

Much like the heart, if we are to be of any use to ourselves—and others!—we must first make sure we are able to be present to what's going on inside. We must be able to listen and really hear and be fully *here* in the moment. Being present and available to yourself means that your mind and body are quietly focused. Your mind is wrapped around the relationship you have with yourself, and your whole being is in harmony with that focus. You are in a state of awareness, a state of mindful presence.

This is precisely how self-care works, and it is accomplished in solitude through meditation, the development of inner peace, ease with your surroundings, and love for others. It is the embodiment of working on yourself, getting to fully understand what makes you tick, and having a rich relationship with the person that is you. It is what allows you to love freely and live fully. Such is the importance of committing to a growth process of self-care and self-awareness!

If you can commit to that, then you can commit to other relationships as well. You can be present with *other* people, and you can offer good care and healthy attention to these relationships. You can be a good friend, a great lover, a wonderful son or daughter or parent. So, in this way, caring for yourself is caring for others. You learn to become all you can be, honestly and genuinely, while seeing through eyes that are focused and hearing through ears that are receptive to the truth.

OBSTACLES TO GROWTH

Life can be *chaotic*. While we're driving, we're thinking of a million things that have to be done once we arrive at our destination. While we're on the phone, we're cooking. While we're in a business meeting, we're thinking about the weekend. Once the weekend comes, we have scores of chores to do in the yard or around the house, or maybe we have to take care of something with the car. We may have things planned with the neighbors or with friends or family—the list goes on and on. It seems almost impossible to get time for oneself, to devote energy to nurturing and preserving our own being.

Maybe we plan a vacation, and once we're there we busy ourselves with the same running, talking, thinking, and doing that we allow to occupy us at home. But now we're doing these things with palm trees in the background or Mickey Mouse ears on our heads. Care and nurturing still don't happen—they just cost more!

Life can be *overwhelming*. When we are not paying attention, we find that the list of day-to-day demands on our schedule, energy, and talents seems to grow of its own volition, totally beyond our scope of conscious awareness: a partner's needs, a child's needs, a parent's needs, tasks to be finished, goals to accomplish, new projects to begin, health issues, work issues, money issues, family issues. When we do stop to take a breath, we wonder, *How did this happen to me?*

I am reminded of the words by Rabindranath Tagore: "The butterfly counts not months but moments and has time enough."

Life does come with a pause button. We just have to remember to push it! We need to remember self-care. We need to remember that in order to love others, we must first love ourselves. We need to remember, first and foremost, our hearts.

THE TRUE SELF

Learning to nurture oneself in everyday living is a way to honor the *true self:* who each of us is in our quiet moments. When we peel off the layers that are sometimes necessary in order to survive in our day-to-day world, we are left with the true self—not the work self that needs to be efficient and task-oriented; not the social self that requires charm and pleasant conversation, whether we feel like conversing or not; not the various other public selves that have to make adjustments many times throughout the day. Once the layers of public selves have been stripped away, each of us is left with our inner person—who we are at our very core—with all its wisdom, serenity, awareness, centeredness, and honest feelings.

The true self is that part of us, that identity, that wears no armor. It stands alone; it sometimes thinks profoundly, and very often it feels deeply. It's what we were born with and what we die with—without all those costumes we wear in between. The true self is the self from which all the others begin. It is the home of our genuineness, and our very humanness. The true self, like a beautiful and valuable flower, needs attention and care.

Meditation is one of the most effective ways for identifying the true self as well as learning techniques of self-nurture. Meditation allows one the quietude and introspection that lets each of us connect with our inner being. Through meditation, we can reach that place of centeredness, that peace, where we find out who we really are. No tests, no deadlines, no facades. When we are alone with and in touch with the inner being, we can actualize our ability to reach toward those places hiding behind the other selves. We can touch our genuineness, our honesty. We can be ourselves. We can simply *be.*

Just by going to that place, we nurture that place. It receives our attention. We are *there.* We are *present.* Nothing is more important. We wrap our minds around it. We engage our hearts. We become fully enraptured in the fine art of being. We come home to ourselves. We breathe. We live. We *are*.

A MEDITATION FOR THE HEART: "FINDING YOUR TRUE SELF"

This meditation may be read slowly by a friend or silently to oneself. I recommend that you do this meditation every few days at first, then whenever you feel the need to reconnect with your center, your true self.

Breathe and enjoy the benefits of the breath. Breathe slowly, rapidly, deeply, or shallowly…however you want. Breathe in order to feel good, alive. Breathe in order to be aware of the breath. Play with your breath. Breathe for the sheer fun of it.

[Pause]

Now let your breath find its own pace. Let your awareness come to the peaceful feeling of simply breathing. Doing absolutely nothing, worrying about nothing. Feeling free. Unencumbered. Just breathe and be.

Breathe and be.

[Pause]

Imagine now that all your responsibilities have vanished. Take your time and think about them, letting each one go. Just let them float away. All your fears are gone. All your worries have evaporated. There is no one demanding anything of you. There is nothing you have to do. Treat yourself to this delicious freedom. Let the feeling, the relaxation, wash over you.

[Pause]

Let yourself be. Simply be. Breathe into just being. Breathe.

Now allow your mind to focus on this thought: I am fully and wholly who I am. I am fully and wholly my truth. Repeat this to yourself several times. I am fully and wholly who I am. I am fully and wholly my truth.

[Long pause]

You are a unique creation.

You have the ability to know yourself as no one else can.

What is your truth?

[Pause]

Make a commitment to yourself that you will get to know your truth more and more each day. You can have all the time you need, for your own awareness, for your own growth. Take the time to nurture yourself. Take the time to know yourself.

Breathe nurturing energy into every cell of your being.

[Pause]

Commit to ever-increasing awareness about who you are. Breathe acceptance into your process.

[Pause]

Commit to nonjudgmental honesty. Breathe and allow yourself unconditional love.

[Pause]

There is no one like you. You are unique.

Breathe in love...wrap this around your heart.

Let your relationship with yourself bloom.

Accept your uniqueness unconditionally. Celebrate your uniqueness.

Celebrate being human.

Celebrate being exactly who you are.

PART TWO
FAMILY AND FRIENDS

For a community to be whole and healthy, it must be based on people's love and concern for each other.
—Millard Fuller

CHAPTER

TEN

My Best Friend's Wedding, Funeral, and Bar Mitzvah

You are always welcome here.
—Mr. Rogers

Good friends may be the most valuable gifts of all. They stand by you; they accept your tears, share in your joys, help you fight your battles, and know you with an intuition based on countless hours spent genuinely listening to you. How many times have you felt blue, discouraged, battered, and when you called up a good friend you started, slowly but surely, to relax, free yourself from stress, absorb the comfort of their company, and eventually rediscover your sense of humor? This is the power of perhaps the best kind of support group: close, dear, valued friends.

There's an intimate relationship between a person's self-esteem and the kinds of friendships he or she has. The effects of nurturing, supportive friendships can be both subtle and obvious, and they contribute positively to a sense of self-worth. Likewise, when a person has nonsupportive relationships in his life, the effects can be quietly insidious or overtly damaging.

This holds true not only for friendships but also for relationships with significant others and family members. In this chapter, several of my personal friends' experiences illustrate what aspects of friendship help nurture self-esteem. (Besides, here's a chance for me to boast a little about a few of my friends, who claim they're not mentioned enough in my books.)

But first, I invite you to take a moment and think about who you consider to be your very best friend. Give the following questions some thought before you proceed.

• What do you get from this person that makes him or her so important to you?
• What are the qualities that mark this friendship, and why do you value these qualities so highly?
• How do you feel about yourself when in the company of your best friend?

Most people have friendships that vary in closeness and intimacy; I like to use the analogy of dropping a stone into a pond. The stone makes ripples of varying sizes in the water, forming multiple inner and outer circles, all of them in motion, in flux. In our friendships too, some people fall into our inner circles and some who fall into the outer ones. There's often movement between circles of friends, as some friends become closer over time and others become more distant.

Now think about some of your other friendships. Imagine someone specifically from an inner circle. How do you feel when you are with this person? Can you imagine life without him or her? What is it that rates a person worthy of your inner circle? What qualities do they possess, and why would you say these qualities are important to you?

What qualities—or lack thereof—would keep a friend in

one of your outer circles and make feeling closer to him or her unappealing? Can you imagine growing closer to this friend? What would that require? What would that be like for you?

In certain support groups that dealt with friendships and support systems, I've used a guided meditation to help members clarify the extent to which they value certain people in their lives—which friends are most important to them and whose friendship they cherish the most and why. There are variations to the exercise, but basically it goes like this:

Imagine talking on the phone with your closest, dearest friend; in the course of that conversation you intuitively become aware that you're talking with your friend for the last time.

What do you want to say to this person, so as to be fully honest and leave no unfinished business between friends?

Give this some thought. Does anything remain unresolved? Or have you been you totally up-to-date with each other, especially about your feelings for each other? Does this person know precisely how you feel about him or her? Are you certain?

How would you close the conversation? Would you say, "I love you"? "Good-bye"? "See ya in the next life"?

You can try this exercise yourself in the quiet of your own home and see what the results are for you.

PUTTING WORDS INTO ACTION

In March 2000, there was a California ballot measure commonly referred to as "the Knight initiative." Officially known as Proposition 22, it was a particularly divisive measure that would have prohibited California from recognizing same-sex marriages that had occurred in other states. The insidiousness of the initiative was that at the time no states in the union had voted to legalize any form of same-sex marriage. The real purpose was to ensure that if any state ever did legitimize gay and lesbian marriages, such unions would not be recognized in California. The slogan for the proposition was "Save Marriage!"—interesting that the thought of legalizing marriage for some is so threatening to others.

A further irony was that the initiative's sponsor, Congressman Pete Knight, was known to have a gay son and a gay brother, and he was not too thrilled about that. Rather than dealing personally with his feelings about his son and brother, Knight proposed a nasty ballot measure that polarized the state and increased the overall level of homophobia as well as the risk of physical assault for gay people. Especially in more rural or conservative areas, Proposition 22 contributed toward creating a very hostile climate for gay people.

Although the proposition was defeated in large, progressive communities with significant gay populations, pretty much everywhere else it passed. The overall margin was approximately 60% for and 40% against, and once the vote was in, conservative newspapers didn't hesitate to run such front-page headlines as "Prop 22 Passes Overwhelmingly!" But the margin by which the initiative was approved had a lot to do with the high-profile grass roots campaign waged on its behalf by the Roman Catholic Church and the Church of Jesus Christ of Latter-day Saints. Homophobic church leaders from those and other denominations handed out thousands of lawn signs to their parishioners, signs that proclaimed PROTECT MARRIAGE— VOTE YES ON PROP 22. Ministers exhorted their parishes and congregations, "You believe in marriage, don't you? Then put these signs out where all your neighbors can see them. And take some extra for your friends." No thinking involved.

The lawn signs were everywhere.

But thinking people who didn't blindly adhere to whatever homophobic messages they were receiving—people who have their own intelligent thoughts about what's going on in the world—weren't buying what the signs promoted.

At a dinner party some good friends and I were discussing the Knight initiative with disgust. Everyone present—the heterosexuals as well as the gay folks—were all intelligent, creative, analytical thinkers, people outraged that this proposition would raise its ugly head in a state as supposedly progressive as California. We all agreed that whatever good might come of the measure would include:

- Opening the doors of discussion about same-sex marriage for years to come and thereby establishing it as a civil rights issue of our time.
- Forcing many people to think through—for the first time perhaps—the wide variety of issues surrounding same-sex marriage, particularly spousal rights and responsibilities, which many heterosexual partners take for granted.
- Encouraging the general population to confront aspects of homosexuality that they were happily keeping behind the shut closet doors of their minds: "Don't ask, don't tell."

In an effort to counter the pro–Prop 22 campaign of the Mormons and the Roman Catholic Church, more progressive churches and organizations created same-sex marriage study guides and sponsored discussion groups. "Committed gay folks want the same rights as married couples? Hmm...maybe we ought to think about this." These groups were encouraging, since they did not spew yet more homophobia but served to open minds and encourage legitimate debate. There was now a very clear target for gays and supporters of gays to add to their political agenda. Same-sex marriage unified people's energy for a new legislative priority and gave every independent thinker something to think about.

I'd like to share with you how one of my friends dealt with this issue after our dinner party. A raving heterosexual and what I call a "thinking Christian," Peg called me and said she felt it was important to do something to make sure her voice was heard. And so she did what I highly recommend people do as a way to take action: something that helps a person feel like she or he makes a difference in this world while enabling others to feel less alone with their own issues of helplessness, oppression, and fear. She wrote about it.

The following is an excerpt from a letter she sent to her local small-town newspaper.

> *The March election has come and gone, and Proposition 22, the proposition that says California will not recognize same-sex marriages, has passed. And while this initiative has stirred considerable discussion statewide, our local published discussion here in the Commonwealth has mainly consisted of the supporters of the proposition airing their views. I am not a proponent of Proposition 22, and while the election is in the past, I hope that the deep thinking, soul searching, and discussion about this issue are just beginning.*
>
> *My thoughts are these: What right is more inalienable than to love whom one chooses? What truth is more self-evident than that all people, no matter what their sexual orientation, are created equal? What commandment, no matter what your religion, is more*

important than love one another? How does ostracizing and denigrating a group of people support that most important of commandments? How does promoting fidelity and commitment between two people, whether they are gay or straight, weaken the institution of marriage? Why should a law legislate whom I love, or whom I (or you) choose to marry?

Gays and lesbians are human beings. Human beings fall in love and want to spend the rest of their lives together. Why should one group of humans not be allowed to formally consecrate and celebrate that love in front of family and friends in a religious ceremony, if they desire. And why shouldn't their union be legally recognized when they have made the same commitments to each other that heterosexual partners have made? No law can legislate away homosexuality. Shouldn't we, as a society, promote and support committed, loving, relationships that build a stable, caring community? At the very least, society's laws should not interfere with anything this deeply personal.

I hope that when my children grow up, this period of time will be looked back on as we now look back on segregation: As a period of deep ignorance from which we have evolved.

Talk about helping to fight important battles! This is but one reason that Peg is in *my* inner circle of friends.

DEVELOPING EMPATHY

A college buddy of mine, Rich, wanted to tell me of a particular experience he had with a former neighbor friend. Rich is married, has two children, and was living in Canada. He has a deaf daughter, so his family is acquainted with others for whom deafness is a part of their lives. Since he'd read my previous book and knew that I often write about self-esteem—the self-esteem of gay people in particular—he felt it important to share his story. He wrote me the following letter:

Dear Rick,

I have a story you might find poignant. This experience made a big impression on me, and I can only say that I have now moved closer to appreciating and empathizing with how hard everyday life can be on gay folks' self-esteem.

While in Toronto, my wife and I became friends with a gay sign-language interpreter named Don. He lived a couple of blocks away and he would often visit us. Don had AIDS and frequently had episodes where he required hospitalization.

Whereas Don lived alone and had only a bike for transportation, one night at 3 A.M. he called me. He needed someone to take him to the emergency room, as he was having serious symptoms and was becoming dehydrated. So I got in my car and picked him up and drove him to the nearest hospital.

He was very sick, so he was understandably frustrated with all the admissions paperwork and formalities. He mouthed off to the nurse and was generally a pretty unpleasant guy. While in the middle of giving his information, he had to run to the rest room and asked me to tell the nurse he had AIDS.

Finally, they admitted him and brought him back and put him on an I.V. I went into the waiting room and tried to stay awake. About 20 minutes later, a

*female nurse came for me saying in a very sarcastic,
cold tone of voice, "His highness wants you..."*

*I was puzzled by the nurse's iciness toward me and
lack of compassion for Don, his bad mood aside. She
led me back to his bed in the E.R. and a couple of times
the nurses would come by, frown and shake their
heads, or ask me to do something for him that maybe
they should have done themselves.*

*Finally, it dawned on me that the medical staff
thought I was Don's partner. I was suddenly aware of
the negative attitude and how far from enlightened
these front-line medical people were. I certainly felt
their scorn even though I was just a neighbor out of my
bed in the middle of the night to help my friend. To be
the object of their contempt really bugged me, but
that's not what was important. I realized that gay people are subject to this discrimination all the time—even
when they are in dire need of medical help.*

Rich wanted to share with me a moment of personal growth
and greater understanding on his part. Although understandably
concerned about what his friend had to endure, the silver lin-
ing, for him, was the new empathy he felt toward the plight of
gay people and persons with AIDS. An independent thinker
and supportive friend committed to his own growth, Rich is one
of my dearest and most valued friends.

Passing the Test

I was having dinner in Los Angeles with my best friend,
Ginger. Her fiancé, Patrick, was joining us for the first time. He
was meeting "the best friend," and I was meeting "the new
beau," someone I figured would become a part of my life and,

hopefully, a pleasant part. Now mind you, this kind of situation has a degree of built-in stress. Sometimes the person your best friend is dating (or in this case plans to marry!) can never stand up to the scrutiny of her family of friends. It's hard: You want what is best for your friend, and that desire often produces unreasonably high expectations: "My best friend is wonderful—who could *possibly* be good enough for her?"

Over dinner Patrick was talking about a married couple who were his friends. Before he got too far into the story, he briefly clarified they were a heterosexual couple. His intention was to show me that he didn't *assume* that a committed couple necessarily consist of a man and a woman—even a married one. Because he was in the presence of a gay man, he knew it would have been insensitive to make such an assumption. In my world, a couple often is a same-sex couple. Patrick realized this and succeeded in weaving this fact into his conversation subtly, sensitively, and without fanfare.

Finally, it seemed that Ginger had met a man whose sensibilities and sensitivity matched her own when it came to matters of sexual identity. While Patrick could just have been on his best behavior because he was meeting the best friend of his wife-to-be, he has displayed the same total lack of homophobia since his marriage to Ginger. Just the other day he was telling me about two friends who live together. It was a few minutes before I caught on they are lesbians—so natural are same-sex couples to him.

I know I have wonderful, exceptional friends. I value them as nothing less than lifelong members of my true, created family. But I also know this is no accident. I don't believe I could have good friends who'd have issues with someone being gay, lesbian, bisexual or transgendered. If you believe in and stand for certain values, then you naturally attract and surround yourself with people who are like-minded, who hold those same values in high regard. While differences of opinion are healthy, and a strong friendship allows room for such differences, the underlying support for who you are and what you are about is never in question in a genuine, supportive relationship. It is, instead, nourished and celebrated!

If those with whom you have chosen to surround yourself display for you a love that is *conditional*, where only certain parts of you are acknowledged and deemed acceptable, then you have people around you who are not necessarily good for your self-esteem. Not being able to be who we genuinely are has been a fundamental injustice heaped upon gay men and lesbians throughout history. As children, we had little choice about who was in our circles. As adults, we have total choice.

When you commit to an emotional closeness with another human being, you commit to a reciprocal interchange of self-esteem within that relationship. *Your feelings of self-worth are reflected in and by that person.* In other words, how highly you think of yourself is illustrated in the people you have around you. Especially if you are gay, this is a most crucial aspect of friendship if you are to embark on a path of improved self-esteem. Choose the people around you wisely.

~

I value my friends as I value myself.

~

I seek friendships that enhance my self-worth.

~

I strive to be the kind of friend I desire.

ELEVEN

DATING WITHOUT ABANDONING

I will bless my neighbor. May my neighbor bless me.
—Celtic prayer

When Walt began seeing his new boyfriend, he was understandably excited. He had been single for over a year and felt unhappy about that, especially during the months before starting his new relationship. He knew better than to rush into a relationship just for the sake of having someone to introduce as his boyfriend, but nevertheless he was feeling lonely and wanted someone special in his life.

In the past Walt may have succumbed to the old untrue adage that "a bad relationship is better than no relationship." He'd had enough therapy to know that simply wasn't true or healthy. In fact, quite the opposite is true: Not being in a relationship is most definitely preferable to being in a bad relationship. While being lonely can be hard for some people to deal with, being abused—physically or emotionally—is deadly to one's self-esteem. Being single offers a person a chance to work on issues that simply do not arise once one is in a relationship. It is a valuable, often-missed opportunity to do some of the personal growth work that eludes those who go right from one relationship to another. I'll offer for purposes of illustration the experience of my friend Grace.

"Getting to Know You"

When Grace was single for perhaps the first time in her adult life, she was extremely lonely and thought she'd never survive the hollow, depressed feelings that plagued her during those first few months. It was very difficult for her, never having been without a girlfriend throughout adulthood. She didn't know how to do it. Always having a companion created for her a kind of emotional safety net where significant personal issues were not demanding her attention. She was always distracted with the attentions and affections of her relationships.

But now, for the first time, it was different. Grace was experiencing something new and alien to her. After those first few months of purposely filling her time with a myriad of other distractions, some healthier than others—renting movies, making long late-night phone calls with friends, shopping, working late at the office and on weekends, traveling to see out-of-state relatives—Grace finally took a breath and took stock of her situation: she was a single gay woman in her late 30s. While she could not at first claim to be happy about that, she realized that she hadn't spent much time getting to know herself very well. She couldn't claim to have been a very good friend to herself, since she had been living a life where she didn't create any opportunities to find out who she was when she was alone and with no one but herself. Quite the opposite was true: She devoted much time to keeping busy, always going somewhere or doing something. Gradually, an aspect of excitement and wonder and discovery began to creep into Grace's awareness as she explored her own landscape of emotions and thoughts like she never had previously.

"It was a little like Christmas," she'd tell me. "Without someone to run off to and find out first and foremost how *they* felt about something, I was left to find out about my *own* thoughts and feelings. How does *Grace* feel about something? That was new. I never really took the time to see what my feelings were in any given situation. It was a kind of laziness I think. How do you feel about...whatever? OK, I'll go along with that."

Grace got to a point where she was hoping *not* to find a girlfriend, at least for a while. She was enjoying her quality time with friends and family and, most importantly, with herself. Her time with others began to feel less and less like a distraction in which she could lose herself and more like an addition to her already full presence. She was liking herself much more as a result of this expansion and awareness of her true self. And as her self-esteem soared, she realized just what a good friend she could be—to others, and to herself. This became a process she relished.

It's no accident that about a year later the woman Grace did meet turned out to be the woman she married. Being more of a whole person in her own right—and *knowing* that person better than she ever had—allowed Grace to attract a woman who complimented who she was, as opposed to someone who could fill in all her missing parts. That's a significant difference—the whole point, really—particularly in regards to unrealistic and misplaced expectations of the other person, and it represented huge personal growth for Grace. Learning to get to know herself may have been the best gift she's ever had.

• • •

Back to Walt. He was now officially becoming part of a couple, and his new relationship was taking most of his time and energy. Whereas he had been spending lots of quality time with a variety of good friends, he was now going on regular dates with Eric. He was enjoying himself very much. But before long, his friends were beginning to grumble about missing him, having to wait longer and longer for Walt to return their calls, complaints that are good-natured and somewhat playful, but reveal an element of truth and some feelings of being neglected. While Walt understood that they missed him and felt even a bit flattered by that, he continued to make his new relationship a priority and found it difficult, if not impossible, to also find time to be with his good friends. The situation was becoming frustrating for all.

While Walt's friends weren't any more demanding than most people would be when missing an important member of their support and/or social circle, there are steps he could take to improve understanding and communication while allaying the hurt feelings of loved ones. Good friends will understand that a new love requires attention, and they must be patient. However, even good friends need attention from time to time, and to suddenly feel that part of one's support group is being redirected away from the fold can cause deep feelings of abandonment.

Even though Walt is the one with the full dance card, he too may feel abandoned because he's no longer enjoying his friends and all the time he once spent with them. The situation creates a kind of void in his life as well. Additionally, friends might begin to plan events without him, as they acclimate to his new schedule and unavailability. Everyone may well understand that this issue is most relevant at the start of something new. As the saying goes, "This too shall pass." But in the meantime, here are some suggestions that were helpful to Walt, and may be helpful to you if you're ever in a similar situation. These suggestions will help maximize the support of friends and minimize hurt feelings all around.

Five Steps to Dating Without Abandoning

Identify Your Close Friends

Take stock of who your friends are, your inner circle of close friends as well as your outer circles of acquaintances. Include family members and work colleagues if you wish. You may even want to illustrate this by drawing concentric circles on a piece of paper and listing on each circle the names of people with whom you enjoy spending time.

Determine Time Spent Together

Before you began dating the "new guy" or "new girl," you probably socialized regularly with some of the people close to you. Consider each friend you used to see on a regular basis and determine how much time you'd spend together each week (or each month).

Determine the Adjustment

Now, how much time are you spending with your new boyfriend or girlfriend each week? That time has to come from somewhere. Which friends are you seeing less often because you're going on dates with the new person? How much less time, exactly, are you spending with these friends? Whom are *you* missing the most?

Compromise

What's a reasonable amount of time you can still allow for your friends while continuing to date as much as you'd like? Are you willing to commit to spending a certain amount of quality time with your friends if you count phone calls as well as in-person meetings? (You can still have great heart-to-hearts on the phone, if not in person.) Maybe you can set aside a regular "phone date" with a friend each week to catch up on each other's lives and share your new excitement.

Communicate

Now call all of your close friends one at a time over the next few days. Discuss with them how you have been thinking of ways in which you can still enjoy time together, even though you have someone new in your life. Let them know your ideas about regular social times and phone calls, even if that quality time needs to be somewhat reduced. See what you can come up with together. In the process, you'll give your friends the message that they are important to you and that you miss them. Such a positive message will undoubtedly contribute to their being more patient and understanding precisely when you may need it the most.

Remember, quality is more important than quantity. When time is at a premium, some close, personal one-on-one time together, even brief, is usually more satisfying than a group event. Eventually you'll want to help your new partner acclimate to your inner circle of friends, since he or she will want to bring you into his or her life too. It's far healthier to bring your new partner into a group of close friends and family members who have been well taken care of by you along the way. Too often, the new guy or new gal is the unfair recipient of hostility, jealousy, or resentment from the gang, all of which is avoidable with some care and forethought on your part.

Walt discovered that by taking the above steps he was able to address any issues he had with his friends before they took hold and became problematic. Walt loved his friends very much and didn't consciously seek to exclude them from this new chapter of his life. By paying attention and focusing on the needs of his established relationships, he was able to incorporate his new relationship into his life with care and thoughtfulness, which helped all his friends gladly make any necessary adjustments.

Other Uses

Similar steps can be taken whenever there is a major life adjustment at hand, such as moving to a new part of town that may be farther away from your friends or family, or starting a new job that suddenly takes up more of your time.

Another common example that requires extra effort and attention is when someone in a group of friends gets married or has a baby. Their life changes completely! With a new baby it is most definitely a period of adjustment for the new parent(s), but also for everyone around them. A newborn necessarily becomes the center of the parents' universe, especially at the beginning, and understanding, support and communication become vital for everyone involved to maintain contact and closeness. Any person could easily feel left out or abandoned. Staying clear about the importance of your support group, together with everyone doing all they can to nurture the friendships in creative ways, become key to celebrating the new life that has entered the picture and to cherish the old solid relationships that surround it. With nurturing, care, and attention, relationships can—and do—last a lifetime.

Richard L. Pimental-Habib, Ph.D.

~

I stay mindful of the people I love.

~

I am committed to nurturing my healthy relationships.

~

I stay whole by keeping close to those I love.

Chapter
TWELVE

HIGH-MAINTENANCE MOTHERS, FATHERS, AND OTHERS

The violets in the mountains have broken the rocks.
—Tennessee Williams

The results of poor parenting fill therapists' offices: people with issues that had begun in childhood and taken firm root, then flourished throughout their adolescence and later caused angst and great emotional and psychic pain during adulthood. These results can range from mild—the normal neuroses of everyday living—to devastating, as in cases of sexual, emotional, or physical abuse.

Emotional abuse is hard to define. What constitutes emotional abuse these days is quite different from what was considered emotionally abusive in years past. Experts nowadays better understand the consequences of poor parenting, largely because of issues that have made their way into the offices of therapists. Parents leave marks on their children in ways both subtle and obvious, whether through lack of interest or loving support, covert neglect, harsh and demeaning words, or psychologically damaging messages.

This is not to say that newfound knowledge about parenting has not led to wonderful changes. It always does my heart good to see a devoted parent with his or her small child in the market or walking together in a park. More than likely, that parent is doing an admirable job of raising a secure, confident, inquisitive, happy child filled with the self-esteem that will be the foundation for a good life ahead. Some adults have had to make a conscious effort at learning good parenting skills; others are just good at it. They shoot from the hip with love and healthy impulses while staying motivated to learn, improve, and grow along the way. I wish I saw more parents like that; unfortunately, I also see parents who don't listen to their children and who become tense and abrupt and thus unknowingly send the child all sorts of negative messages about conditional love and self-worth. Whenever I see that, I think how I'd like to give that kid my card; he may really need it in 10 or 20 years.

In this chapter, I want to share a few stories about clients (and one friend) with whom I've had the privilege of working. They are all brave, healing people, and it has been humbling for me to join them on their paths of life for whatever duration of time. They have consistently confirmed the power of committing to one's process and the tremendous growth available to those who believe in the road toward self-awareness.

DEREK

I want to introduce you to a client who is a recovering alcoholic, one of many I've known who has been fighting with addictions of one sort or another. He was doing quite well with sobriety, in spite of being fairly new at abstinence, taking one day at a time as his program teaches. And although I've known countless people—personally as well as professionally—with "difficult" mothers, this man had a mother who provided some exceptionally tough challenges. During his recovery he became painfully aware of how profoundly difficult she could be.

It was a hot summer day in Southern California, and Derek was hosting his mother during her visit from the Michigan. She was there for a week and was staying with her only son at his apartment. Derek had recently moved to California to get away from the strictures of his small hometown as well as his parents' home. To hear him tell it, his mother had never been especially supportive of his being gay, and she had made it difficult for him to come out not only to her but also his other relatives. She'd say things like, "Oh, don't tell your father. It'll kill him." Another one of her stock expressions was, "No one else needs to know. I'm embarrassed enough for everyone." Charming.

It hadn't been easy for Derek. He had hoped that, if his mother visited him on *his* new turf, she'd be more understanding or open than if he visited *her* back home. At the very least she'd be on her best behavior, right? Well, hope springs eternal.

Derek's mother knew her son was a recovering alcoholic, but she wasn't overtly supportive of his efforts toward sobriety. The family as a whole enjoyed drinking, and several relatives regularly misused or abused alcohol. Supporting anyone's effort at a sober lifestyle didn't come easily for this mother. One day while they were having lunch at an outdoor café in a beach town, Derek and his mother had this conversation:

Mother: It's so hot here today. I don't know why you like living here.
Derek: It's even hotter in Detroit, mother.
Mother: Well, what shall we have for lunch?
Derek: I'm going to order some iced tea.

Mother: Don't you want a nice cold beer?

Derek: No, I don't. I'm sober, remember?

Mother: Oh, Derek. One drink won't hurt. What are they teaching you at those meetings? You can't have one drink with your mother?

Derek: No, mother. I'll have the tea.

Mother: Oh, for God's sake—well, I'll have a nice, cold, frosty beer. Order one for me. I'll be right back.

Derek's mother, as we can see, is the very antithesis of supportive. In this story, she comes across as either clueless or cruel. Or both. As she goes off to the rest room, Derek is left to not only order a tall, cold beer on this hot summer day but also to sit there with it at the table while waiting for his mother to return. Once she comes back she dramatically relishes the taste of her beer while forcing Derek to test the strength of his recovery program.

In the course of working with Derek, I was impressed with his ability to handle his mother's lack of supportiveness during the week she visited, especially since they have a long history of difficulty together. What may not be evident to an outsider is often painfully clear to the person whose buttons are being pushed left and right, buttons only a mother (or other significant relationship from childhood) can push. What may look like nothing to a casual observer can be enormously infuriating and hurtful when it's really about old wounds being reopened and old disappointments being relived.

I asked Derek about his ways of coping with this kind of frustration.

Dr. Rick: What's it like for you when she is obtuse about all your hard work with sobriety?

Derek: First, I get this stabbing annoyance, like a flare of anger. She's done this my whole life: been clueless, not tuned in at all to what's important to me, or what I'm going through.

Dr. Rick: So this cluelessness is an old familiar theme.

Derek: Definitely. My entire life, all through school, career, boyfriends...

Dr. Rick: But that doesn't mean you're not angry when it happens.

Derek: Exactly. She still pushes my buttons.

Dr. Rick: So now it's about alcohol, but her lack of understanding—

Derek: Is across the board. The subject doesn't matter. It's who she is.

Dr. Rick: It sounds like you're trying to accept and understand *her*.

Derek: I'm trying to accept that she's not going to change.

Dr. Rick: OK. So how are you coping with it this week while she's here?

Derek: I've found that it doesn't do me any good to let her get to me. It gives her so much power over me. This is simply who she is. She's a very limited woman.

Dr. Rick: So understanding her limitations helps you manage your anger at her?

Derek: Yeah, it's getting better. I just don't want her to control me anymore. She's controlled me my whole life. So I try now to just let it go, let it roll off my back.

Dr. Rick: How do you do that? For instance, when she wanted you to have a beer with her—she really pushed for you to have that drink.

Derek: I take a deep breath, realize who I'm dealing with, and get very direct with her: "No, Mother." It usually works. She backs off.

Dr. Rick: And how does it feel when it works?

Derek: Like I'm an adult. I'm not a kid she can control any-more. I'm my own person. It feels really good to stand up to her. It's exhausting work, you have to always be on your toes, but it feels good when it works.

Dr. Rick: You're taking back your power.

Derek: [*smiling*] Yes, I guess I am.

While Derek's mother was *not* any more supportive simply because she was on his turf, he found out that he was better able to handle the challenges she regularly posed because of her lack of awareness and understanding. This is perhaps the most beneficial result to arise from her visit: Derek's newfound ability to handle the disappointment and anger he feels when in her company. Realizing he has greater coping skills gives him confidence to handle not only his mother but others who may remind him of her—partners, friends, employers—whoever brings up the echoes of his relationship with her.

It's easiest to pick on mothers. Let's face it: They are most often the primary child care providers and can therefore pro-foundly influence a person's psychological makeup for better or worse. But fathers and other people instrumental in a person's upbringing—stepparents, grandparents, siblings—can pose a similar degree of challenge. I have a friend who was raised by a much older brother, and her childhood was a nightmare. The majority of her issues today stem from those formative years with her brother, himself heavily influenced by an inadequate upbringing. Emotional baggage left over from childhood is really about who can push your buttons.

Undoing emotional damage from childhood is a lot of work, but it can be accomplished. It's important to remember that healing is a process, especially when it feels like it's happening too slowly. Whatever may have happened to you in an earlier chapter of life had many years to begin, develop, and take hold; these issues won't be healed overnight.

LONNIE

I had the privilege of knowing a dear friend, Lonnie, who had a terrible emotionally abusive childhood. Raised without a mother, he suffered at the hands of an inconsistent, unpredictable, violent father who was an alcoholic. Lonnie moved out as soon as he was able, at age 18, and has been working on his self-esteem, spiritual growth, and emotional healing ever since. One of the many damaging things he was taught as a child was that he was worthless—an extremely difficult message to overcome. As a young adult he chose partners who kept treating him poorly, a dynamic with which he was all too familiar. Through ongoing therapy he began to turn this—and other destructive behaviors—around.

Lonnie worked in HIV education and was devoted to teaching others how to take good care of themselves. Ironically, he was very good at his job. He could help *others* to be well and prioritize their sense of self-worth, but he had not learned to value *himself*. One thing Lonnie enjoyed was nature, particularly beautiful flowers. As part of his healing process, he started to put a big bouquet of fresh flowers in his apartment every week. This was a great extravagance for him, but he decided that having fresh-cut flowers in his environment was worth cutting corners someplace else in his budget—his happiness was worth it. Each Sunday he'd walk to the corner florist and purchase a big new batch of fragrant blooms. He loved to come home to their smell, their color, their sheer beauty. The flowers helped him feel alive, vibrant, and connected with nature. They carried a big, empowering message: *I'm worth it!*

For Lonnie, that Sunday walk to the florist was like a warm, comforting hug. He hadn't gotten many hugs in his childhood; for him, the flowers were healing.

JANINE

Another former client of mine, Janine, received a powerful message similar to Lonnie's throughout her childhood: *You're not good enough.* This message took various forms: *You're not doing well enough in school; you're not being helpful enough with your siblings; you're not pretty enough; you're not making us proud enough.* Janine didn't feel loved; she felt regularly denigrated. Life is hard and stressful life when such a memory deeply informs all you do and say as an adult. Trying to exist with these wounds is exhausting, let alone trying to repair this kind of damaged self-esteem. A person really misses out on life when his or her whole focus is about pleasing others. Ironically, Janine's efforts to please were what contributed to people *disliking* her and being annoyed—rather than pleased—with her. Here's an important lesson:

Each time we act for the approval of others, we put ourselves in a state of anxiety and dependence. We are dependent on others' acceptance and anxious that we won't get it.

Read those two sentences again. Now take a moment and think about whom *you* feel the need to please. Ask yourself the following questions:

- Who is the first person to come to mind?
- Are you aware of the anxiety you feel when you're with this person?

- Are you aware of your anger toward this person?
- How strong would you say is your dependence on pleasing this person?
- Can you remember when this need to please first began?
- Are you aware of how much effort and energy this requires of you?

It's exhausting to be vigilant about the happiness of others at your expense. It requires your constant attention, without which your perceived failings can all too easily catch you by surprise, causing you to feel overwhelmed, frustrated, and depressed. It's a psychological ball and chain, and at the more disabling end of the spectrum, it can cause people to be severely depressed and experience ulcers, heart attacks, or strokes.

For Janine, these feelings of anxiety and the accompanying state of dependency were a regular experience. She felt this way whenever she was around people, her coworkers and bosses in particular. She held a very responsible position in a law firm and had both a significant other and children. The demands on her time and talents were extraordinary. In addition, she did volunteer work that was very important to her spiritual well-being, but lately she was feeling overwhelmed and unrewarded. It felt as if there simply wasn't enough of her to go around. Although she wasn't willing to give up any part of her life, she understood that she couldn't keep up her juggling act without increasing her level of stress and experiencing a decline in health as well as increased moodiness, anxiety, depression, and a general lack of enjoyment of her life—even those aspects of it that gave her some pleasure.

Janine needed to get in touch with the source of her motivations. She needed to ask herself why was she so determined to be the best at everything she did and to please everyone with whom she came in contact. Sometimes she complained that she felt "like a hamster on a treadmill in a cage. You go and go all the time, doing what you are supposed to do and never really getting anywhere." It was no wonder she felt this way, given the tremendous pressure in her life. But it was a result of not just the life she'd created but also her beliefs about herself, based on what she had been taught: *You're not good enough, so try harder.* Remember those childhood messages she'd received? She needed to be the best, and she needed everyone around her to be pleased. She felt *responsible* for everyone else's happiness. She needed to feel in control of her work, her family—indeed, making sure everyone liked her was something she thought she could control.

In recovery programs, participants learn there are three things they cannot control: people, things, and events. That was a hard pill to swallow for Janine because her early childhood messages left her feeling so powerless, so impotent, that she had to get a handle on herself and her world and everyone in it. So she tried very hard for many years to be in control until she started to break down. And that's the moment when healing began.

It was a long healing process for Janine, but with psychotherapy, support groups, self-help books, and seminars—she worked as hard at her process as she had at everything else!—and the support of an understanding partner and family, she was able to change her perception of herself as well as identify and deal with her anger and unhealthy motivations. Eventually, Janine began to let go of her need to control her world so rigidly. She began to understand that she really wasn't in control of other people at all; instead, she began to view herself in partnership with others—a significant participant but not always the commanding high ruler. She began to realize that her need to control was anger-based and arose from her childhood. It had caused to her to miss out on too many joys: her children growing up, her partner's career achievements, her family's special occasions. Ultimately she saw that the messages she'd received as a child were just plain wrong. She learned to affirm that she *was* enough. She was smart, attractive, accomplished, competent; she was plenty!

And most important, she discovered she was lovable—and loved.

There is always hope. No matter what messages you received during *your* wonder years, there is a way—a way that's best for you—to work through the emotional fallout from dealing with a challenging parent or having had a difficult childhood. A high-maintenance mother, father, sibling, grandparent, or stepparent is not a yoke around your neck under which you must suffer your whole life. The process of healing old wounds begins with your desire to lead a better life—a happier, more fulfilling life, whatever that may mean to you. That desire and an accompanying commitment to your own well-being is the first step, and it's half the battle really. Only you can make such a commitment; only you can enter into whatever process is best for you, understanding that while healing does not happen overnight, it does happen.

And you deserve it.

~

I am not doomed to a life of being a victim.

~

I am not controlled by my past.

~

I am on the road to freedom.

CHAPTER

THIRTEEN

AUNT ROSE, IT'S NOT A DAMN CHOICE!

To thine own self be true.
—William Shakespeare

Dear Aunt Rose,

Notice that the ones who shout the loudest about homosexuality being a choice are always straight? Such experts they must be.

What the heterosexual, homophobic, right-wing, deeply ignorant, fear-based, faux-Christian contingent of our society consistently fail to realize is that homosexuality is not, never has been, and never will be a choice. You don't wake up on Monday and decide to be gay because it goes better with your outfit. Then, on Tuesday you feel like polyester, so it would be much better to be straight. Wednesday's a rayon day—that's a toss-up.

Being a Republican, however, is a choice—as is being a bigot or a religious fundamentalist.

You know about these right-wing homophobic types— they're the ones who always complain about being labeled "homophobe" because they don't agree with the "liberal viewpoint" or the "homosexual agenda." They like to hide behind the cloak of Americanism or God and turn the tables on labels, spewing homophobia even louder when their righteous conservatism is threatened. I wonder how would they feel if suddenly by a majority vote they were denied one of their basic rights because of their choice to be right-wing homophobic Republicans? Let's say the right to be legally married.

Denying legal marriage to right-wing homophobic Republicans would mean:

- *They would be denied the income tax break offered to married people when there's only one working partner, or a partner making significantly less money. (The IRS considers same-sex partners with disparate incomes to be single people, who pay taxes at a higher rate.)*
- *They would be denied the nontaxed spousal benefits offered to married partners by virtually all large employers. Even if they worked for one of the 3,400 employers that extend health insurance benefits to domestic partners, Uncle Sam counts such benefits as taxable income.*
- *They would be denied the automatic right to sue for damages on behalf of their partner following accidental death or injury. There would also be problems with social security benefits should one partner die while the children are young, or if one parent dies. And estate taxes would be a nightmare.*
- *They would also lack public recognition and support for their intimate relationships; they would have to fight for joint child custody while fighting the sneers and protests of their married counterparts; they would not automatically inherit from a deceased spouse under probate laws; they could not share auto and homeowners' insurance policies at reduced rates; and they would not have imme-*

diate access to their loved one in case of accident or emer-gency.

- *And there's bound to be some stupid military policy to deal with.*

Oh, sure...it's a choice. So I say, let them choose discrimi-nation. See how they like it.

LOUIS

When a client of mine, Louis, decided to come out to his family, he knew he'd be facing some very potent homophobia and ignorance. "This is not a family that keeps up with the times," he kept telling me. As far as he knew, no one else in the family had ever come out. At least no one had ever spoken of such a thing—not in his family.

His family lives in an outlying suburban area of Los Angeles and has a long history of citrus farming, a lost profession in Southern California's fast-growing urban sprawl. Although Louis considered his family loving, hardworking, and honest, he's been clear about their lack of sophistication when it comes to topics outside of immediate family concerns, which centered around health, heterosexual family occasions, church, and their farming business. Getting to know about their gay son's life, friends, lovers, and interests would definitely stretch their level of tolerance and usual ways of thinking. Louis realized this prior to coming to them, even although he already was out to his friends, colleagues, and acquaintances.

Louis is in his early 30s and a professional writer who free-lances for several gay magazines. He lives in Los Angeles and has many friends, both gay and straight, and for the most part is quite content with who he is and where he's heading in life, both personally and professionally. Although still single, he has experienced enough counseling to have an understanding of his personal strengths and weaknesses and accepts both with a sense of humor and lighthearted charm that makes him enjoyable to be around and easy to know. He's been a good friend to his friends and is basically a happy, generous, motivated, self-aware guy.

Louis has evolved quite far beyond the boundaries of his family's limitations, both psychologically and professionally. He's worked hard at it. So when Louis decided to come out to them, he began with his brother, Tom. He and Tom had always been very close during childhood, and have remained close, despite geographical distance and differing directions in life. One night over dinner, Louis told Tom he was gay. Tom's reaction was fairly subdued; he claimed he'd "suspected" it but hadn't wanted to say anything, feeling it was none of his business. He said he loved Louis the same whether he was gay or straight. "It really wasn't a big deal to him," says Louis. "He's the most open-minded of the brood, however."

"But," he continued, "Tom strongly advised me not to say anything to our parents, or our aunt and uncle for that matter, which wasn't really a shock. None of us [six siblings] thinks that their generation would even know how to begin to understand me." Louis eventually worked his way through his other siblings, mostly with very positive results. "Even when my sister had a difficult reaction, she still reminded me that she loves me and accepts whoever I am. It was a very encouraging process."

Louis's situation highlights a very real issue for many gay people who are out in *almost* all aspects of their social and professional lives. A snag that is both psychological and practical, however, occurs in that area of life where one is not out; remaining closeted, in some particular environment or with certain people precisely because they perceive great difficulties otherwise. This kind of challenge crosses socioeconomic, political, professional and personal lines—it can, and does, happen to many.

COMING-OUT ANXIETY

It's easy—and quite common—to experience impatience and anxiety when approaching the time of coming out to important people in your life. The more important the person is to you, the more anxious you may be. There's a lot on the line. And in your imagination, there may be even more on the line. The anticipation of rejection contains a lot of emotional and psychic distress. It's pretty much the reason people stay in the closet: rejection of one form or another.

One thing to remember, however, is that the difficulties you anticipate are almost always worse in your imagination than they turn out to be in real life—not always, but almost always. One factor here is your own ability to intuit as honestly and objectively as possible another person's response, which is less of an unknown if you know the person well and have a history with him or her. Perhaps an indication may be how unpredictable the receiver of the news is as well as his or her religious background, general level of open-mindedness, and anything he or she has already said about gay people.

What often gets in the way of the courage needed to come out is your own impatience with the listener's potential reaction to the news. You can be more helpful if you are more patient with the listener. Think how long it took you to accept yourself; perhaps you can better understand someone needing a bit of time to let the news of your sexual orientation sink in and to make the necessary attitude changes to better accept and understand you. The more the surprise, the more time they may need. The less the surprise, the more some of the groundwork has been laid, consciously or unconsciously.

When I talk with parents of gay sons or daughters, they all agree this much is true: *How someone feels at first upon hearing the news that a loved one is gay is not how they will feel later on after they've had a little time to acclimate to the idea.*

LIVING HONESTLY

Coming-out stories are as unique as every individual. Yet despite all the personal trials and tribulations, they all have something in common: Each denotes a gay person who was motivated to live honestly, to be accepted unconditionally, and to break out of hiding. Some people take those things for granted; gay people cannot.

The time has never been better, historically speaking, for the coming-out process, with benefits both individual and collective. In large urban centers and small towns alike, there are brave, intelligent, history-making men and women who are paving the way in politics, the arts, and our schools. At the time of this writing, there are 24 major characters on television who are openly gay or lesbian. Twenty-four out of hundreds isn't much, but compared to last year, five years ago, 20 years ago— progress is definitely humming along in Hollywood. (In an unprecedented accomplishment, *Will & Grace* won three Emmys this year!) With a few steps forward and an occasional step backward, we are becoming more visible. Fewer and fewer people in our society can claim to not know a gay person, and that is precisely how ignorance is diminished.

So, as the worldview of homosexuality is in slow transition, we are perhaps more able to view the world as a place in which to come out. Not all small communities are hostile toward gays, nor are all religions. Gay life no longer has to exist only in big cities; progress is being made in smaller towns as well. It's certainly true that large metropolitan areas regularly have more to offer—socially, spiritually, educationally, artistically, and domestically—for gay men and lesbians, but more gay people are desirous of returning to their non-urban roots. They find that someone they went to high school with is now an "out" lesbian and is leading a productive and fulfilling life, accepted and supported by those who know her. Or they find that a new community health center in town has a well-funded HIV program or an outreach program for sexually-active youth. Or they notice a popular gay student union at the near-by community college that sponsors workshops, socials, and speakers. Not all gay activities in all suburban and rural areas take place at the rest stop along the highway just outside of town. Progress is being made slowly. There is hope.

It's important to remember that a growing and significant influence in the education of the masses regarding homosexuality is largely due to the very act of coming out. Over and over I hear straight people say that once a gay person came out to them, they had to challenge and discard many previously held beliefs about gays. Gay people, not only those in the Hollywood limelight or playing characters on television, but also those leading honest, self-accepting, low-profile lives contribute enormously to the changing climate for gays and lesbians everywhere. It doesn't happen over night, and the attitudes and behavior of nongay people cannot be magically transformed in an instant. But greater acceptance does happen consistently, one person at a time, and at each individual's own pace.

Which brings us back to the story of Louis.

When Louis ran into difficulties with his parents and others of their generation in his family, he was able to identify that the primary issue was around their belief that homosexuality is a choice. The more liberal thinkers in his family understood that it is *not* a choice, it is not a "preference." It is a sexual *orientation*, a sexual *identity*, just like heterosexuality and bisexuality. But the more "staunch, old-school, conservative Republican members of my family"—his parents, an aunt, and a grandfather—were convinced that being gay was a choice, and a damn poor, unchristian one at that.

Needless to say, this degree of homophobia posed a challenge to Louis, someone who interacts regularly with people who are well-educated, psychologically-savvy, and pro-gay. To help his family try to better understand his lifestyle, he provided them with pamphlets and several good books about being gay and invited them to attend a meeting of PFLAG (Parents, Family and Friends of Lesbians and Gays). But all his efforts met with a range of feelings from mild skepticism to open disdain. He did his best to remain patient, however, and let his parents, aunts, and grandfather know that if they ever had any questions, he would be happy to talk with them further. Unfortunately, none of them took him up on his offer.

This left Louis with some unresolved anger. It's one thing to encounter the occasional homophobe on the street, since hopefully you won't have to deal with that person on a regular basis. And really, a homophobic comment or show of ignorance is not about the gay person at all; it's about the ignorance. Most gay people learn by necessity to develop a bit of a thick skin. This becomes a harder task, however, when the ignorance lies within your own family, among people you care about and love.

WRITING IT OUT

As part of Louis's therapy in his ongoing process to become more and more the person he wishes to be, he began using his formidable writing talents to deal with his anger. He kept a journal of his experiences about coming out and focused on expressing his feelings. One of his writing exercises took the form of a letter, unsent, to his Aunt Rose. It is the letter you read at the start of this chapter. That letter became the inspiration for a larger article he wrote about coming out for a magazine. But most significantly, what Louis discovered for the first time was that the act of writing helped him to confirm his own beliefs and feelings about being gay. It reminded him of what he believed to be true for himself, and also provided an outlet for his passion. His feelings were able to take flight—feelings of anger, outrage, hurt, envy, regret, fear and more—without any negative consequences. The free expression of those feelings greatly benefitted him. He realized that his own acceptance of being gay was hard-won. And even if he was unable to convince others that sexual orientation is not a choice, he was able to reconfirm his own rightness through his writing.

Perhaps you have some feelings relating to coming out, being gay, or not being accepted or understood by family members or others. Writing down your feelings, as Louis found, can be a highly therapeutic way to freely express your innermost emotions and thoughts. Whether in the form of a diary or letters, such self-expression is a valuable part of the healing process; it provides a constructive outlet and prevents bottled-up feelings from building up and boiling over. Whether or not you mail a letter such as Louis's is not the point. Writing it is something to do for your own mental health and well-being. It can diffuse your impatience, calm your anxiety, center your feelings, and reconfirm your rightful place in the world. It is a gift you give to yourself.

We cannot *change* other people. We can, however, inform and enlighten others' beliefs and perceptions by being fully and wholly ourselves. Our example is what makes an impression—really, the strongest impression.

If you choose to use writing as a constructive, creative outlet for your feelings, then perhaps, like Louis, you'll find the process therapeutic and helpful. Some find expression through art, or by volunteering with youth, or helping the elderly. You read earlier in this book about a friend of mine who expressed herself by writing to the editors of her local newspaper. Some write to their local, state, and national politicians. Some call neighbors, organize petitions, and protest injustices in whatever way is meaningful to them. Every motion matters. Every time you are genuinely and unapologetically yourself, change begins.

~

I celebrate all of who I am.

~

I am creative, unique, and worthy.

~

I am lovable just by being who I am, at this very moment, in this very place.

Fourteen

Out At Work
(Or, My Boss Is a Raging Het)

*The Bible contains six admonishments to homosexuals and
362 to heterosexuals. This doesn't mean that God doesn't
love heterosexuals; it's just that they need more supervision.*
—Lynn Lavner, comedienne

For gay, lesbian, bisexual, and transgendered people, the
workplace environment is one of the remaining "sexual revolution
frontiers"—those areas of society that are as likely to be supportive of members of sexual minorities as hostile toward them, overtly or covertly. Like churches and schools, the workplace is an
arena where we must learn to accurately assess the level of acceptance of gay people as well as the overall environment of fairness.

Our personal sense of worth depends upon being in a supportive environment no matter where we are: work, school,
church, social settings, or home. We spend much of our day at
work—a third of our lives, actually. Our level of comfort with
being out about our gay sexual orientation can contribute to
developing and maintaining a healthy degree of self-esteem, or
it can be damaging because of the cumulative negative effects
of needing to remain in the closet.

Give some thought to your place of employment. How gay-supportive is your boss in both words and actions? How about your colleagues? Do you feel comfortable around them as an out lesbian or gay man? What can you ascertain from bits of conversation overheard around the water cooler (which these days looks a lot like an espresso machine) about the general level of acceptance at your job for gay and lesbian employees?

More concretely, what kind of policy, if any, has your employer put in writing that ensures the safety and protects the rights of gay, lesbian, bisexual, and transgendered people?

Would you be comfortable bringing a same-sex partner to a weekend company event? Has anyone there ever done so? Would there be negative repercussions, subtle or otherwise, on Monday morning, following a Saturday night party or Sunday brunch at the boss's home?

Are you out at work? Is anyone else? Why or why not? Would it be professionally risky to be out? Is there a feeling, something unspoken, about not "flaunting" one's (homo)sexual identity at the office? Or has something to that effect been said to you? If you brought your boyfriend or girlfriend to the office and introduced him or her as such, what do you imagine would be the repercussions?

As to health care benefits, is your employer keeping up with the ever-growing national trend of large companies that offer domestic partner health benefits? More than 3,000 companies nationwide now do so. The majority are, as you might imagine, located in urban settings.

You deserve to feel comfortable where you work. And you deserve to have a productive, healthy relationship with your employer and your fellow employees, free of any tension based upon bigotry or homophobia. So let's turn the tables for a moment. In the spirit of useless, excessive, and time-consuming

E-mails, paperwork, memos, forms, and questionnaires many bosses seem so fond of, I present you with a most *useful* questionnaire.

THE HETEROSEXUAL QUESTIONNAIRE

1. What do you believe caused your heterosexuality? Did you have an overly controlling father and a distant mother?

2. When did you first decide you were heterosexual? How did you know? Are you a practicing heterosexual now?

3. Is it possible that your heterosexuality is just a phase you may grow out of?

4. Is it possible that your heterosexuality stems from a neurotic fear of others of the same sex?

5. If you have never slept with a person of the same sex, is it possible that all you need is a good gay lover?

6. Do your parents know that you are straight? Do your friends and/or roommates know?

7. Why do you insist on flaunting your heterosexuality? Can't you just be who you are and keep it quiet? And why do you need parades?

8. Why do you heterosexuals place so much emphasis on sex?

9. Why do heterosexuals feel so compelled to introduce others to their lifestyle?

10. A disproportionate majority of child molesters are heterosexual. Do you consider it safe to expose children to heterosexual teachers?

11. How can men and women know how to please each other since they are so anatomically different?

12. With all the societal support marriage receives, the divorce rate is spiraling—it's now up to 51% in the U.S. Why do heterosexuals have so few stable relationships?

13. Statistics show that lesbians have the lowest rate of acquiring sexually transmitted diseases. Do you feel it is really safe for a woman to maintain a heterosexual lifestyle and run the risk of disease and pregnancy?
14. How can you expect to become a whole person if you limit yourself to compulsive, exclusive heterosexuality?
15. Considering the global menace of overpopulation, how could the human race survive if everyone were hetero sexual?
16. There seem to be very few happy heterosexuals. Techniques have been developed that might enable you to change if you really want to. Have you ever consid ered aversion therapy?
17. Would you want your child to be heterosexual, know ing the problems she or he would face in society?
18. Do you think God approves of your heterosexual lifestyle?

Do you have an employer who needs to read this? Do you have colleagues who *just don't get it*? My friend and colleague, Terry, always asks about my partner whenever she sees me. We may be in the middle of an office environment or a social gathering and just as naturally as she asks about someone's husband or wife, she asks about my lover. And knowing that I am out to all, she doesn't hesitate to ask, regardless of who may be near, nor does she lower her voice just a bit, as others do, as if protecting a secret. To her, a spouse is a spouse, whether heterosexual or homosexual. She's a good example of someone who gets it.

Another friend of mine has several sets of godparents for her children. One set is an older married couple; one set is a divorced interracial couple who are still friends, and one set is a gay couple. She, too, gets it. She wants her children to benefit from the wisdom of their elders and learn to celebrate and cherish diversity in all people. These kids will grow up to be wonderful employers or employees, enriching the workplace with their ability to value all human beings. They will have relationships with others based upon mutual interests and an openness to learning, not based on age, race or sexual orientation.

A "Belongingness" Meditation

Some people did not have a safe childhood. They weren't able to feel safe at home, at school, or with certain adults—authority figures and perhaps even family members. There was not place in their world where they could go to feel comfortable, secure, and unconditionally loved. Therefore, they weren't able to feel safe even within themselves. This is certainly—and unfortunately—true for many gay people.

As adults, many gay, lesbian, bisexual, and transgendered people do not feel safe where they live, where they work, with society at large, or within their own families. *One cannot thrive or be creative or successful when one feels continually threatened.*

Whether you had a safe or unsafe childhood, it is important that you feel safe now as an adult in your home as well as your place of employment. It is reparative to understand that you are *worthy* of safe relationships and of living a life in which you feel you belong, where the rightness of who you are and your place in the world is not questioned but accepted, even celebrated—especially by you! It's a journey that begins with you. So I close this chapter with a meditation that I hope you will find to be valuable in maintaining your self-worth.

This meditation is also very helpful when you want to feel better connected to yourself and to others. Sometimes it's easy to feel disoriented or disenfranchised from the world, especially for members of a sexual minority. Confusion, alienation, and feeling as if you don't belong can come more easily than a spiritual or emotional connection, particularly during times of stress or depression. And that's when we need our center the most. Try this meditation whenever you need to feel centered within yourself, and more engaged with the universe.

If you did the meditation in chapter 2, then you'll know that there is no right or wrong way to do this (or any) meditation. Just relax, breathe, and allow yourself to be. You belong. You deserve this.

This following meditation may be read slowly by a friend or silently to oneself.

Take several deep breaths. As you breathe, focus on your given right to your breath. You are human, you require—and deserve—your breath.

[Pause]

As you breathe, think about your body. Become aware of how every part of your body is connected to every other part. This body is yours. It is alive. It is a part of all things living. The planet is affected because you are here, breathing and alive.

[Pause]

As you breathe, think about your mind. Your mind is central to who you are. With your mind you make choices every day that begin chain reactions throughout humankind. Your choices touch others directly or indirectly. Your choices matter.

[Pause]

You breathe, you live, you matter. You occupy space and time.

You interact. Your aliveness is uniquely yours, yet connected to all other things.

Now let yourself focus on a positive, joyous, significant relationship in your life. This may be a relationship from the past or present. Visualize yourself engaging with this person.

[Pause]

Now let yourself experience the rich fabric of feelings that come with a meaningful encounter with this person. Enjoy all the warm and positive feelings attached to this relationship. Let yourself fill up with the goodness, the happiness, the contentment.

[Pause]

As you have your feelings, bring this understanding into the picture: I deserve this.

[Pause]

Let these words resonate in your mind loud and clear: I am fundamentally as good a person as I can be right now, in this moment of my life. I am a work in progress. I am deserving of love because I am human. I am deserving of happiness, because I am human. I deserve to be here, side by side, with all other living creatures. This world is my home too.

[Pause]

Repeat these thoughts hourly, daily, weekly…whenever you desire to feel a spiritual oneness with your world. Whenever you need to feel you belong.

You belong here. This is your home too.

You are alive.

You matter.

PART THREE

THERAPY

*The real voyage of discovery consists not in seeking
new landscapes, but in having new eyes.*
—Marcel Proust

FIFTEEN

MOVING ON:
HEALING AFTER A BREAKUP OR DEATH

There is release from anguish in action.
—Frank Lloyd Wright

It's a fact of life that everything ends. I remember a curmudgeonly uncle of mine saying that there are two things we can always count on: death and taxes. I don't think he was the first to say that, but he sure liked to quote it. And the saying holds some truth: Death of all things, of all people, is inevitable.

Perhaps accepting that fact—through literature, art, storytelling, even from watching the daily news—is a way human beings have of unconsciously attempting to prepare, each in our own way and time, for the inevitable. We know it's coming, and to ease our existential angst over its impending occurrence, we desensitize ourselves to the reality of it. We read about it, we talk about it, we fret over it. Among the most emotionally charged vignettes in our collective unconscious is the Death Scene, à la *Romeo and Juliet.* We stop and look at accidents along the freeway to reassure ourselves that we aren't the ones

171

lying over there on the asphalt but someone else. Whew...

More important, an acceptance of the end of things, if done in a healthy fashion, is a way to encourage ourselves to live more fully. Life is short. It is often the death of a loved one that drives that lesson home. A close personal loss changes a person for life. Will it be for the better or for the worse? That, I believe, is up to you.

As with all other living things, relationships eventually end, either by running their course or because of the death of the other person. Regardless of what brings about the end of a relationship, there are qualities of grief, as well as tasks for the grieving person to work through, that are similar. This chapter focuses on the emotional and psychological implications of endings, whether the end is the result of a breakup or death.

What we're dealing with here is the end of a significant loving relationship, be it family, lover, or friend, and for some people this can be a topic that is extremely difficult to deal with. The pain around endings can be great, and healing depends largely upon three key factors:

- the circumstances that led to the ending
- the surviving individual's level of coping skills
- the (perceived) support one receives at that time

Let's take a brief look at these factors, beginning with circumstances. Some deaths occur after a prolonged suffering, and some happen tragically without warning. There are ways these two types of loss feel different to survivors, provide different obstacles to healing, and require different kinds of coping. Likewise, the end of a relationship because of a breakup can seem to come out of left field, or it can be the final result of a long, emotionally battering struggle. The exact circumstances of a breakup usually lie somewhere in between these two extremes. Different ways of breaking up can all feel different too and leave a limitless variety of scars on our hearts—some deep and long-lasting, some more easily soothed.

What were the last words spoken? What were the last deeds done? Were the two parties *current* with each other, saying all they needed to, or is there important unfinished business left to deal with? Were there arguments and hurt feelings, or love and warmth? The moments (days, weeks, months) before an ending may be the strongest memories after the ending, and they can last forever.

When it comes to coping, everyone's coping skills are different. Some of us have an ability to take on the burdens of the world and survive quite well—psychologically intact and with more valuable life lessons accumulated and embraced. Others with limited tools for coping have a harder time with daily stressors, let alone the loss of a loved one. Most of us are somewhere in the middle, but coping styles and strategies are indeed unique to every individual. If this is a first significant loss for you, it's new ground—you haven't had to deal with this before, and it may be understandably frightening, confusing, and overwhelming.

One of the most important factors in healing from a loss is a person's support system, or more specifically, their *perceived* support system. It doesn't matter if everyone they know is calling, E-mailing, or stopping by with condolences. What matters is if the bereaved individual is *feeling* supported. All the home-made postmemorial service casseroles in the world may not help, but perhaps a phone call each evening from a good friend will. Meeting new people may feel like a burden, but meeting deadlines at work may be just the ticket. It all depends on what the individual perceives as supportive and recuperative, whether that means staying active or lying inert, talking with others or shutting down for a while, or taking long, hot bubble baths or long naps. A good friend will try to ascertain what is needed or wanted, and will attempt to provide exactly that. When in doubt, it's quite OK to ask the following questions. "What would you like me to do to help?" "Shall I come over, or shall I give you some space?" "May I check in with you each day by phone, or would you like to call me whenever you feel up to it?" These are questions that can really help a person with support and kindness. Whether that person knows what would feel good or is too confused to even answer, he or she at least knows you're available. And that in itself can provide a degree of healing.

An important word of advice if you are trying to help a grieving friend: Stay away from the "shoulds." "Should-ing" on others says more about you than provides help to them. For instance, "You *should* go out and meet new people" is illustrative of your discomfort with your friend staying home alone. "You *should* get back to work" says that you are uncomfortable with the length of your friend's recovery time and want him or her to get back among the living. Well, that may work best for you in a similar situation, but is not necessarily what is best for them. You can't know. Your friend may barely know, especially during a time of grief. So cut your friend some slack. If you "should" on him or her, you're in the way. You're there to help, to assist with your friend's ever-changing, sometimes confusing, and often unpredictable needs, not to direct a production of his or her healing process. If this is difficult for you, you might ask yourself: *What is my patience level? Why does their response to loss make me uncomfortable? What is my own relationship to loss?*

I hope you will stay with this discussion of grief, as difficult and emotion-packed a topic as it is, since there is much to learn from it, perhaps something that will help you if you are presently coping with a loss, or have a significant loss in your past, or perhaps are wanting to help a friend through his or her loss. More than anything, grief provides an opportunity for you to explore your own relationship to loss. Take a deep breath and absorb what you can—what you are *ready* to absorb—and save the rest for another time. It's OK to deal with life in increments, as we are able. In fact, the stages of grief illustrate this very point.

THE THREE STAGES OF GRIEF

It's generally accepted there are three major stages of grief that one goes through when mourning a loss. (This is not to be confused with DABDA—denial, anger, bargaining, depression, acceptance—the stages of dying as formulated by Dr. Elisabeth Kübler-Ross.) Distinct from Dr. Kübler-Ross's concepts, the three stages of grief are:

- Shock and Denial
- The Letdown
- Acclimation and Accommodation

These stages and their characteristics are not written in stone. They may overlap; the bereaved individual may go back and forth between them, and each stage may look—and *feel* — quite different to different people. So the most we can do is to try to form a basic understanding while keeping in mind that if you are grieving, it's common to experience these stages.

Shock and Denial

This stage refers to that stunned initial feeling summed up in the words, "I can't believe she's (or he's) gone," after someone's death, or in the case of a breakup, "I can't believe it's over." It seems unreal, like it didn't happen, couldn't possibly have happened. You'll wake up tomorrow and it'll all have been a bad dream. Some people I've worked with in bereavement counseling describe this time as walking through a haze or a fog—they feel distant from everything, looking around but not really seeing anything. If you've experienced a significant loss in your life, you undoubtedly know well what this is like.

In this stage, denial can take many forms but generally shows itself in a refusal to fully believe that your loved one is gone or that your relationship with him or her is over. The unconscious likes to play tricks during this stage: You'll swear you just heard his voice in the next room or saw her driving in traffic. Many clients of mine have expressed expectations such as fully expecting the ex to come home from work at 6 P.M., just as he did every day when they were still together. In dreams, the loved one is often alive. This stage can be confusing, painful, and even disorienting. So know this: Denial gets a bad rap. It's there for a very good reason, as it forms a kind of protective curtain which parts only long enough to let in the amount of reality we can handle. It's a necessary device for coping with pain.

The Letdown

I call this next stage the letdown, because it's when depression is likely to set in. The above-mentioned protective curtain of denial is lifted. It has served its purpose, and now it's time to deal with the truth: the partner is gone. If you know someone who's at this stage and trying to deal with the reality of their loss, it's important to keep an eye on them. If one has a tendency to be suicidal, this is when they are at highest risk. If one is sober, this is the stage that will challenge their sobriety. People often experience a rush of feelings during this stage that can threaten to overwhelm their coping abilities. It's a tough place to be. Good friends—and good listeners—are very valuable during this time.

Acclimation and Accommodation

When you get used to the loss—i.e., when you have accepted it to the best of your current ability and begin to approach life again—then you are trying on a new identity, a new way of seeing the world and yourself. It may be a smooth transition or a difficult one, depending on the factors mentioned earlier. You may take a few steps back into the letdown, or even denial, as you progress slowly in fits and starts, a couple of steps forward, then a step or two backward. However it goes, you are gradually acclimating yourself, internally, to a different life, a partnerless life. Passing the restaurant on the corner may still bring back a strong memory of eating there together, but at least you can drive by it now without falling apart. Sure, the songs are sad and movies touch you deeper than you knew they could—but you are surviving these feelings, sometimes even welcoming them. You are acclimating.

"Accommodation" refers to developing a life in which you accommodate this new identity, this state of being single, of being the one left behind. You take care of the chores, you pick up the slack, you strengthen your independence. Eventually, you'll get out of the house and start seeing other people socially. When friends ask how you are, you'll say OK and mean it. You'll begin to develop a stronger sense of yourself, your abilities, your changed life. Will you still miss your ex? Of course. For a while, maybe forever. Once you have experienced a personal loss, you are different and always will be, in ways both overt and subtle. But at this stage of your process you will have gathered up enough of your inner resources to know that eventually you do have to move on if you are to remain among the living. Again, depending on the factors mentioned earlier, this stage may take some time to reach—for some it lasts only for weeks; for others, years. That part doesn't matter, although the earlier stages don't necessarily feel good. What matters most is that you reach this stage in your own time and are not pressured by the "shoulds" of others so that you arrive here safely and intact.

HELPFUL TIPS FOR HEALING FROM LOSS

Several insights about healing have emerged as tried-and-true tips for negotiating the murky emotional, psychological, and spiritual waters of loss. These helpful tips have grown out of my years working with clients grieving a death, loss, or life change as well as various seminars, workshops, and grief groups I've facilitated. If there's any field where people can learn from each other, it's the field of bereavement. Everyone does it differently, and learning what works for others can be quite valuable. I've learned much from the clients with whom I've had the privilege of walking such a journey. I offer these findings to you, along with some of my observations based on clinical study and personal experience, to help you as you work through your own losses and endings.

Normalizing Feelings

It's important to be in touch with your feelings. Specifically, it's important to *normalize* your feelings. What that means is that your feelings are yours, and they are valid. Even more, they are *indicators* for you; feelings inform you of what's happening personally and specifically for you that requires your attention. When addressing feelings, keep the following in mind:

- If you're depressed, ask yourself about anger. What are you angry about, and are not expressing at this moment?

Also, *who* are you angry with? Why?

- If you're angry, ask yourself about fear. What are you afraid of? What is frightening you right now?
- If you're sitting with sorrow, what about your world is disappointing you? *Who* has disappointed you?
- If you're emotionally shut down, it's for good reason. What has happened that you don't feel you're able to deal with? It's OK to deal with it at a later time; for now it is healthy just to identify it.

Asking yourself the above questions is a helpful exercise whether or not you are dealing with a specific loss. These feelings arise all the time; the point is to be aware of them, and to understand what message they are giving you.

Too often we judge ourselves: We feel guilty if we feel relief or happiness after a loss. We think we're not sad enough, not depressed enough. Or we feel guilty about feeling angry at someone who left us. It's OK to feel fear. It's OK to feel numb or shut down. It's OK to feel anything. Feelings are feelings, and they are earned and justified. It is simply unhealthy—and unhelpful to your grieving process—to judge your feelings based on others' preconceived notions (or your own harsh condemnation) of which feelings are appropriate for grief.

They all are!

Remember: If you're sad, you're sad about *something*, whether or not you can identify that something right away. So rest assured there's a good reason you're sad. If you're angry, that's perfectly natural. In grief work, I tell my clients that "where there is loss, there is anger." It's earned. It's yours. And it's important to get in touch with that anger. If you're depressed, have a good cry and really feel depressed. It's valid. You deserve it! When we bottle up our feelings and not allow ourselves to work through them we get into all sorts of trouble—both psychologically and physically. Don't let others "should" on you about your feelings, and don't "should" on yourself either!

The Year of Firsts

In the field of bereavement we refer to the first year after the loss as "The Year of Firsts"—the first Christmas, birthday, or anniversary without your partner. It's your first time going to the movies alone. It's your first Sunday brunch alone, whereas before you usually got together with three other couples. It's your first trip to the market, your first trip back home, or your first summer vacation that your partner is not there to help plan. Even if *you* wanted the breakup, that doesn't mean that you won't be experiencing emotional repercussions from the ending. You'll still be reminded of places, events, and little personal things—those things that were private between the two of you. It wasn't all bad. Even if it's healthier for you to be without a partner, you may still miss him or her.

How can you get through the year of firsts? If possible, plan ahead. If you know an occasion is coming up, think about how you want to spend that day. Alone? With friends? With family? The day will come, and the day will pass. You'll survive it, especially if you can take care of yourself and your needs during that time. It's important to allow yourself the attention and nurturing you need. This isn't business as usual—it's a special time and requires special attention.

Different Types of Loss

Let's face it: There are many different types of loss. If your grandfather's beloved pet has been his best friend for 20 years and has provided him cherished company and suddenly dies, should his feelings be less severe than that of someone who recently experienced the breakup of a one-year relationship? How do you gauge loss? Who is to decide where each individual falls on the grieving meter? I've known people who needed to grieve the loss of a celebrity, whereas others didn't shed more than a few tears after the dissolution of a 10-year relationship. Grief is an individual process.

MULTIPLE LOSS

Before you get through the emotional and psychological fallout from one loss, *wham!*—you're hit with another. That's multiple loss. The important point is that each loss needs to be grieved. If you don't fully process your feelings after the death of your father, then the next time you break up with someone, it'll have all the punch of that breakup *and* your father's death. If you don't allow yourself to grieve that, then the next loss will be layered on top again. Eventually, the weight of unresolved grief will keep you from getting close to anyone, as your emotional world will feel too precarious to do so. This is one reason why people shut down emotionally and avoid intimacy.

SUPPORT, COMFORT, NURTURING

What do you need? Sometimes during grief it's hard to know. So try different things. Make an appointment with a grief counselor; call a friend; go to church; go to the beach; stay under the covers; take a bubble bath; take the dog for a walk; meditate; write down your thoughts and feelings in a "healing diary"; rent movies; cry; laugh; scream into your pillow; surround yourself with his or her pictures; listen to sad songs; ask for hugs; drink milk straight from the carton; have ice cream for breakfast; join a support group so you can see that others are going through all the same things you are. Once you figure out what you need, even as those needs change from moment to moment, ask for it. Those close to you want to help you heal, but they can't read your mind. Ask as often as you must.

Moving On

Disabled veterans advocate Harold Russell once said, "It is not what you have lost but what you have left that counts." When you begin to feel that way and truly believe it with your mind as well as your heart, then you are beginning to heal. You are experiencing the gratitude for what is left in your life and the people still in your life. You learn to treasure all your relationships.

When you move into the stage of acclimation/accommodation, one of the healthiest ways to accommodate to the loss into your life is through volunteering to help others. Now that you know what it's like, you may be of great comfort to others who are going through difficult times too—even if their difficult times are *different* than yours were. When you feel like you have something to offer other people, you know that you are incorporating your loss into your identity.

Whether or not you actually volunteer, the feeling that you *could* help others indicates that you in fact have enough internal resources to give some away. You've moved from feeling mostly emptiness to that place of starting to have your whole self back again. Slowly but surely, you feel less hollow. You may feel you're a different person than you used to be—and that's very true. You are now a person with a painful loss in your past—but you are nonetheless a person again. You are healing. You are moving on.

~

I am surviving.

~

I am healing without judgment or agenda.

~

I will live to love again.

CHAPTER

SIXTEEN

WHAT IF...?

There are situations in which hope and fear run
together, in which they mutually destroy one another
and lose themselves in a dull indifference.
— Johann Wolfgang von Goethe

Ever play the game What If...? when you were a kid? You know: What if you won a million dollars? What if you found out you were adopted? What if your parents suddenly moved to a new town? What if your annoying little brother went to live with Aunt Pearl and Uncle Bob? The hypothetical questions were meant to be sometimes humorous, sometimes frightening, and usually thought-provoking, depending on the age of the players, of course.

Here's a version of the What If...? game for the gay adult. Sure, you could use these questions as a party game, but they are really about getting to a place where you allow yourself to be introspective and meditate on topics not usually thought about during the course of our busy days. These questions are intended to help you get in touch with what you value, who you are, and who you are in relationship to others.

Take your time with these questions, perhaps taking turns

as you read them aloud with your partner and share your answers with each other. Consider writing down your answers and looking at them six months from now, then a year from now and even five years from now. Naturally, you can do this exercise by yourself and use it as a tool for individual growth. But the exercise is ideal for opening lines of communication between yourself and your mate, or between yourself and a parent, a sibling, or a good friend.

Again, be sure to be vigilantly honest with yourself. When you allow for complete and unedited honesty, some of your answers and what they reveal about your belief system may surprise even you. None of us live in a world where honesty is always rewarded, especially after entering adulthood. (Who wants to hear if s/he *really* looks fat in that outfit?) But with yourself, honesty equals growth.

WHAT IF...?

- What if you could be granted one spectacular, magical wish with no negative repercussion whatsoever...what would it be?
- What if you could alter one physical characteristic of yourself...what would it be?
- What if you could alter one physical characteristic of your partner...what would it be?
- What if you could alter one personality trait of yourself...what would it be?
- What if you could alter one personality trait of your partner what would it be?
- What if you had the power to stop aging at any point in your life up to the present...how old would you want to remain?

- What if you could repeat your very first sexual experience, but change one thing about it...what would you change?
- What if you could repeat any one year of your life, without changing a thing, which year would you relive?
- What if you could secretly spend one whole night alone with anyone you desire...whom would you choose?
- What if you were stranded on a tropical island with one platonic friend for the rest of your life...whom would you choose?
- What if you could "unknow" one thing you now know...what would that be?
- What if you could give your partner anything in the world...what would you give?
- What if you could give your best friend anything in the world...what would you give?
- What if you could give a relative anything in the world...who would you choose and what would you give?
- What if you could see your mother only one more time and were granted one minute to say anything you wanted while she remained silent...what would you say?
- What if you could see your father only one more time, and were granted one minute to say anything you want while he remains silent...what would you say?
- What if you could say any one sentence to our current president...what would you say?
- What if you could ask God one question...what would you ask?
- What if you could eliminate just one specific form of prejudice from our planet...what would it be?
- What if you could eliminate one disease from our planet...what would it be?

- What if you could control tomorrow's headlines...what would they read?
- What if you could host a dinner party for four people from history...whom would you invite?
- What if you could host a dinner party for four people currently living...whom would you invite?
- What if you could receive a letter (or E-mail) today from whomever you wish...who would it be and what would it say?
- What if you were to be given an award tomorrow for something you have accomplished in your life...what would it be for?
- What if you were to be given an award tomorrow for some *imagined* accomplishment...what would it be for?
- What if you could pick one destination to spend the rest of your life with your lover...where would you go?
- What if you could read your lover's mind...would you want to? Why or why not?
- What if your lover could read your mind for 10 seconds...what would you want to be thinking?
- What if you could undo one "wild" thing from your past...what would it be?
- What if you could redo one "wild" thing from your past...what would it be?
- What if you could unsay one thing from your past...what would it be?
- What if you could eliminate one event from history...what event would you choose and why?
- What if you could give your mate one trait s/he does not currently possess...what would that trait be?
- What if you could change any one thing about yourself, but only for a day...what would you change?

- What if you could choose whether to be homosexual, heterosexual, or bisexual...which would you choose?
- What if you could pick someone else's parents to be your own...whose would you pick, and why?
- What if you could create or discover one thing to make life easier for you...what would it be?
- What if you could be forgiven for one thing you've done that hurt someone you love...what would it be?
- What if you could teach your partner one thing...what would you teach him or her?
- What if you could pick an actor—living or dead—to play you in the story of your life...whom would you pick?
- What if you could control how to spend your last day alive...how would you spend it?
- What if you could choose the last thing you'll see before you die...what would it be?
- What if you could pick one person to read your private diary after you die...whom would you pick?
- What if you could inscribe your own gravestone...what would you write?
- What if you would be remembered for one thing only...what would you want to be remembered for?
- What if you could choose one last thing to say to one last person before you die...what would you say and to whom?

• • •

Any surprises? Did you learn anything about yourself or your partner? How do you feel? What has this process been like for you?

When it comes to personal growth, there are many ways to

increase your self-awareness and your level of insight into your own needs, desires, likes, dislikes, issues, problems, thoughts, and feelings. Individual psychotherapy, therapy groups, and various kinds of relationship and family counseling can all be helpful in achieving personal growth. Self-help resources—books, tapes, lectures, workshops, support groups, retreats—can be valuable as well. Meditation and hypnotherapy can be highly effective additions to whatever therapeutic choices a person (or couple) may make. Whatever form your process takes, be patient with yourself. Remember, you are a work in progress!

May you enjoy a lifelong journey of valuable and insightful personal discovery and greater self-awareness to enrich your relationship with others, and most important, to enrich your relationship with yourself.

~

My hopes, my dreams, my fears—
they are mine, and they are valid.

~

I participate in the healing of my world, my relationships,
and myself.

~

I can be whoever I desire to be.
I can do whatever I wish.

CHAPTER
SEVENTEEN

RELATIONSHIP MEDITATIONS, PART ONE

Without the still point, there is no dance.
—T.S. Eliot

There are many roads to a successful relationship, and they all begin with a relationship with yourself. And that's the beauty of meditation: It helps you get to know yourself—your thoughts, feelings, dreams, fears, strengths, weaknesses, drives, insecurities, areas of empowerment, points of suffering, hopes for the future, and pains of the past.

Why refamiliarize yourself with pains from the past? Well, first of all, if you still have pain from the past, you haven't successfully worked through those particular issues. Perhaps you've run from them; perhaps you haven't known how to courageously walk through them and emerge as a healthier, fuller individual. Second, in working through past issues we are freed to move forward with our lives; we feel less encumbered and develop healthier ways of connecting with others and more satisfying approaches to loving and living. Without knowledge of who we have been, we cannot know who we are, or the possibilities for who we might become. Without a bold and honest look at our past relationships, we cannot avoid repeating the same mistakes, nor escape the hold of unhealthy patterns.

Knowing yourself allows for a fuller knowing of another individual. A richer relationship with a significant other, really with *all* those around you who come into your life, whether briefly or for the long term, requires you to be freed of your own *stuff*, the obstacles that get in your way of being genuinely and fully invested with others. In love relationships, family relationships, and platonic friendships, we are able to move toward emotional intimacy when we are unburdened by our relationship issues. Everyone's made mistakes; we need not be crippled by the past. We can learn from the past and create new, healthier ways of relating to each other. Meditation is but one tool along that journey.

Remember: Knowledge *is* power. Ignorance does *not* lead to bliss. It leads to feeling stuck and remaining unaware of yourself and your needs; you feel frustrated, helpless, limited. Our degree of inner knowledge—as well as our intuition—can be developed and nurtured, and holds the key to happiness, a content life with a clear direction and guided by sound judgment and confidence. This self-awareness allows you to trust yourself more fully and to learn to rely upon your own intuitive inner wisdom. Your development of self-awareness is the key to staying well, safe, happy, and free to create and explore—you, your relationships, your entire life!

A Meditation for Self-Awareness: "Guardian Spirit"

This first meditation allows you to begin to develop your inner wisdom. It's particularly valuable, therefore, in the development of a relationship with yourself. It's longer than the other meditations in this book, so make sure you're physically comfortable and take your time with the relaxing breaths at the beginning. As with the others, this meditation can be read to you slowly by a friend or you can record it in your own voice. It can be experienced alone or with a partner.

Close your eyes and take several deep breaths. Let your focus come to your breath. Allow your body and mind to slow down. Relax completely. Let yourself have this time free of worry, free of stress...you are filled with relaxation and your breath.

[Pause]

Know that the very act of breathing is something you can trust. It is within your power to breathe however your body may need to. Let yourself breathe calmness into your body. Let yourself breathe peace into your mind. Let yourself breathe in a wonderful, all-encompassing sense of safety.

[Pause]

Now let your mind travel back in your life, to those times when you felt most safe. To those places where you felt secure and free. To those ages when all was well with your world. Try and identify these moments of safety, of happiness, of belongingness. Let them arise clearly and naturally.

[Long pause]

Perhaps you were able to recall many moments from your past. Perhaps you were unable to recall any. Whether many, some, or none, you are now an adult and can enter into a process whereby you can create such moments for yourself.

Using the power of your mind, we are going to create safety.

Using the power of your mind, we are going to develop your inner wisdom and strength. We are going to open a pathway of creative mental clarity and self-awareness.

Safety, inner wisdom, awareness: Let these concepts become real to you.

Safety, inner wisdom, awareness.

[Pause]

I invite you now to create your own safe place. This may be a place from your past, or it can be a place from your present. It may be real or imagined. It's entirely up to you. You can use this same place as a haven each time you meditate, or you can change it every time.

There is but one guiding objective to this place: It must be somewhere that you feel safe, secure, and entirely at peace.

Take a few moments now to decide on your safe place.

[Long pause]

Very good. Now let yourself be there totally, completely. Use the power of your mind to make this place real. What sounds do you hear? What colors do you see? What is the temperature? How does your skin feel? What is above you? What is beneath you? What textures surround you? What do you smell? Are you alone?

[Pause]

Emotionally, how do you feel? Are you happy? Ecstatic? Contemplative? Peaceful? Melancholy? Do you feel centered and quiet? Excited and energetic? Whatever feelings you are having, make them real. Own them. Experience them now. Surround yourself with them. Allow yourself to fill up with them.

[Pause]

Why did you choose this place? What about this place brings up the feelings you are now having? What does this place mean to you?

[Pause]

Being in this place enables you to feel safe. You can trust that here you are safe. This is something that you can count on. You brought yourself here, and here you are filled with a sense that all is well within, and without. Your inner world as well as your outer world both are safe. You are at peace. You are in harmony mentally, physically, and spiritually.

Know this.

Own this.

Feel this.

[Pause]

Now I invite you to begin to discover a distinct yet comforting sense that you are not alone. In fact, you are experiencing a greater and greater awareness that there is a wondrous, benevolent being near you, slowly but surely approaching your safe place. Gently coming closer.

And you smile, as if to welcome its presence.

[Pause]

This one spiritual being coming to you—purposely and only to you—as if you were meant to meet here all along.

It is as if some all-knowing inner part of you, a part that is connected to the entire universe and all living creatures, has led you to be right here, right now at this very moment of your life in this very spot. And it is here and now that you will finally meet your Guardian Spirit.

[Pause]

This benevolent entity comes closer to you now so that you begin to make out a gentle, white fog swirling about. It begins to take shape. It smiles at you...the most radiant and unconditional smile you've ever seen. It welcomes you with an outstretched hand. You reach out.

Hand in hand, you look into each other's eyes. And in the eyes of your Guardian Spirit you see reflected back to you all the pain and sorrow, all the joy and happiness, of your entire life. This Spirit knows you.

And accepts you.

And loves you.

[Pause]

This Spirit wants for you all the goodness in the world and everything you need. And this Spirit wants to help you unconditionally, asking nothing in return.... Your Guardian Spirit wants to be close by your side and deep within your heart.

[Pause]

Now you look down and see that your Guardian Spirit is holding something for you...a beautiful wooden box covered with inlays of your favorite precious stones. Your Guardian Spirit is handing you this most enchanting box.

Intuitively, you know that this box contains exactly what you need in your life right now at this very moment. It contains that which you need more than anything else.

Without any words passing between you, you have the knowledge that this is the gift for which you've been waiting.

Whether this gift is actually small enough to fit in this box, or whether it is an intangible that cannot be contained, seen, or touched...this is what you've been missing, what you've been longing for, sometimes without even knowing it

And your Guardian Spirit has brought it to you now.

You reach out and take the box. You open it. A brilliant white light radiates from within, bathing you in its beauty and comfort. You let it surround you. You feel its power, its grace.

And as the light fades, there it is. There is your gift, specially and uniquely for you. Here it is at last.

[Long pause]

Did you know that you needed this gift? Has it been missing in your life for very long? Has your awareness of this gift— and its absence—been at the forefront of your mind, or has it been buried deep below your conscious thought?

How do you feel now that it is with you? Let yourself have this experience. Let yourself have your feelings.

[Pause]

And as you look up, you see your Guardian Spirit smiling.

And slowly, as before, you see a swirling fog as your Guardian Spirit now gently retreats, leaving your place to once again be only yours, your personal domain of safety. The place of kindheartedness and tenderness.

Your Guardian Spirit leaves as gracefully as it entered.

And you know intuitively that your Guardian Spirit will return, will be present any time you desire. You've only to close your eyes and imagine it.

Your connection to this Guardian Spirit is strong and unconditional.

You will forever have the presence of your Guardian Spirit within you.

[Pause]

When you are ready, you may open your eyes.

A MEDITATION FOR SELF-LOVE: "THE CHILD WITHIN"

Like the above exercise, this meditation also helps you develop a relationship with yourself; specifically, a forgiving relationship with the child you once were. This is an exercise in reparation—repairing the early damage that may have led to difficulties in your adult relationships. The focus is on forgiveness and love, two of the ingredients that contribute enormously to improved self-esteem and greater self-acceptance.

This meditation may be read slowly by a friend or silently to yourself.

Breathe deeply and slowly several times, allowing your mind and body to relax with each breath...in with fresh, cool, clean air, and out with stress. Let your focus be on the relax-

ing quality of each and every breath, so important to the harmony of your body and mind.

[Pause]

Let your thoughts arise and then let them float away on a breeze. Let your feelings arise, filling whatever space they need. You are open to your feelings, feelings that are within you for very good reasons.

These feelings may be understood by you, although perhaps some are not. But they are yours...as much a part of you as is your breath.

There's no need to judge them—just have them, let them be with you. There is no right or wrong to your feelings. Simply accept them. Witness them.

[Pause]

Open up, both to the feelings you enjoy and the ones that make you uncomfortable. What are your feelings telling you now?

[Pause]

Take them all in and give them all the space, all the time they deserve. They are yours, and no one can take them from you. It is OK to feel.

[Long pause]

Now I invite you to see yourself as a small child, with the thoughts and feelings of a small child. How old are you? Where are you? Let your memory place you at a certain place and time. Make this real with the power of your mind.

[Pause]

What are your small-child feelings? Which are the ones you enjoy? When did you first feel them? What do you believe contributes to you feeling this way?

[Pause]

Which feelings are the ones that make you uncomfortable?

When did you first feel them? And why are these feelings with you?

[Pause]

What would you like to say to this small child?

How would you like to say it?

What gift would you like to give him or her?

How would you help this child to feel like the most important, worthy, welcomed, loved person in the world? Do it now.

[Pause]

Let your heart open to this child.

Let your heart open to yourself.

Forgiveness.

Let yourself be forgiven.

Let yourself feel adored.

Let yourself be worth everything.

Let yourself be loved.

CHAPTER
EIGHTEEN

RELATIONSHIP MEDITATIONS, PART TWO

*Life teaches us to be less harsh with ourselves
and with others.*
—Johann Wolfgang von Goethe

In this chapter you'll experience meditations that focus on your relationship with others. Much like the meditations in the previous chapter, however, there is significant attention paid to you, including your thoughts and feelings about yourself. As mentioned early in this book, there can be no relationship with others without a conscious awareness about your relationship with yourself. And perhaps the reverse is true as well. Here's an alternative way of thinking about relationships:

In Eastern philosophy, the concept of "personality" is very different from our Western theories. From ancient times, Eastern philosophy has taught that a whole person consists in part of one's self-definition, the creation and emergence of the self, but that self is always seen in the context of another, particularly a partner or mate. The two parts—yin and yang—make up the whole. You are defined not only in and of yourself but also with another. It's an interesting concept that's amply illustrated in the way your significant other mirrors back to you who you are. The good, the bad, and the ugly are reflected back to us in the eyes of our loved ones, and perhaps in this way we are continually defined and redefined in the context of our relationships.

AWARENESS MEDITATION: "RELATIONSHIP ISSUES"

This meditation may be read slowly by a friend or silently to yourself. Consider having someone read it to you and your partner together.

Sit very comfortably, arms by your side and legs uncrossed. Let cushions or pillows support your body so that you have no work to do in keeping yourself comfortable.

Breathe deeply several times, allowing your mind and body to fully relax.

Focus on the slowing down of your thoughts as you breathe— let them become like sand settling on the deep ocean floor. Quieting, calming, settling.

[Pause]

Let your mind be wide open. Free yourself from troubles and stress. Breathe into a peaceful place. At peace with yourself, your world, and everyone in it.

[Pause]

Now let your heart open also.

In feeling relaxed, let yourself feel generous, kind, under-standing. Be open to the feelings and thoughts of others. Feel generosity. Feel willingness.

[Pause]

Identify for yourself the central relationship issue presently in your life.

Perhaps it revolves around a love relationship. Perhaps it is a family relationship. Perhaps it is with a friend. Whatever is utmost on your mind, let it emerge now.

[Pause]
See this issue clearly and fully. Look at it from all angles imaginable. Look at it from other points of view. Look at it from his or her point of view, free of judgment, free of agenda. Let your mind wrap around this issue completely. And breathe.

[Pause]
Now ask yourself to be open to all solutions and possibilities. What answers emerge for you about this relationship issue? Let them flow, let them come to you fully...with heightened sensitivity and awareness. Stay understanding, stay loving. Breathe.

[Long pause]
What are you feeling now?
What are you feeling toward this relationship, this person?
What are you feeling toward yourself?
Breathe deeply. Stay with an open heart. Stay with love.

[Pause]
Can you commit to the discovery of answers, repeatedly, until you find the one that is best for you both?

Can you come back to this place whenever you desire, being trustful of your increasing ability to find the solutions you need?

Can you allow your innate creativity to emerge? Make that commitment to yourself now.

[Pause]
Breathe and know you are human.

You are a growing, evolving, loving human being. Your possibilities are endless. Your potential is eternal. Your ability to form loving, caring, generous relationships is boundless.

You have the ability to emerge from discord with your heart intact, with your relationship strong.

You have an ability to love yourself and therefore to love others.

You have an ability to love others and therefore yourself.
[Pause]
When you are ready, take a deep, centering breath.

AWARENESS MEDITATION: "RELATIONSHIP QUALITIES"
This meditation can be read slowly by a friend or silently to yourself.

Take several deep breaths and allow your mind and body to relax fully.
[Pause]
I invite you to think of a significant relationship, one that is currently in your life.
Who is this person to you?
Who are you to this person?
[Pause]
Is this relationship one of willful choice or cosmic chance?
What are the positive aspects to this relationship?
What does s/he bring to this relationship?
What qualities do you bring to the relationship?
[Pause]
Now I want you to think of a significant relationship from your past.
[Pause]
Why is this person no longer in your life?
Your choice?
His or her choice?
Chance?
What was positive about that relationship? What was negative?
Do you miss this person? Why or why not?
[Pause]

Now picture yourself in the context of your family. Think of a recent family event, the first one that comes to mind.

[Pause]

How did you feel about yourself that day?

How did you feel about your body?

Your intellect?

Your personality?

Your sexuality?

[Pause]

See yourself now in the context of friendships. Go in your mind to a recent time you spent with a good friend or friends.

[Pause]

How did you feel about yourself then?

Your body?

Your mind?

Your personality?

Your sexuality?

[Pause]

Take a deep breath and spend a few moments flipping through the pages of your history, your own personal scrapbook, and identify all the healthy relationships in your life, past and present.

[Long pause]

Why have these, in particular, come to mind? What is positive about them?

Are there any similarities among them?

[Pause]

Take another deep breath. Now create in your mind a list of characteristics that you very much desire in a love relationship.

[Pause]

Why are these qualities so important to you?

Which of these qualities are present in your current relationships and friendships?

Are they rare to you or found in abundance in your life?

Are they qualities that you yourself possess?

[Pause]

You desire these qualities in a relationship, so ask yourself now: Am I ready for such a relationship? Am I ready to accept these qualities in a lover? How will I contribute? How will I participate in its nurturing?

[Long pause]

What are you willing to do in order to bring such a relationship into your life, or to create room for these qualities in your present relationship?

[Pause]

When you are ready, take a deep, centering breath.

CHAPTER

NINETEEN

DEAR DR. RICK

I have ended by finding sacred the disorder of my spirit.
—Arthur Rimbaud

Over the years, I have written several advice columns for various publications, most often for gay magazines and newspapers whose readers write in with a wide variety of issues. It's been very interesting for me to see how the issues of greatest concern have evolved over time. There was a long period when HIV medications, alternative treatments, and emotional support were concerns on everyone's mind. Then, as the face of HIV changed and people were living longer with the disease, folks were suddenly dealing with everyday life issues that they weren't so sure they would be facing just a few years earlier. Acute health and medical topics took a backseat, and day-to-day living moved to the fore.

I've received questions not only from lesbian, gay, bisexual and transgendered people but also from family members of gay people as well as caregivers, mental health workers, and concerned friends. More recently, as gay men and lesbians are starting their own families, many folks have parenting and adoption questions. Indeed, for many gay people, care giving has become a spectrum of intergenerational topics: parenting our children, caring for our aging parents, and continuing to see to our own general well-being and ongoing life issues. Collectively speaking, we gay people have a variety of very specific concerns to address as we become more visible to the world, more demanding of our hard-earned and deserved rights as equal human beings, and better able to confront gay-related issues in employment, educational, and religious settings.

On the other hand, we are everywhere, in every walk of life imaginable, and our concerns as gay people very often mirror the concerns of mainstream America: familial relationships, friendships, romantic involvements, sex, money, business, success, travel, stress, health...on and on. These are topics that cross the boundaries of sexual-identity, ethnicity, and generation.

In this chapter I have included a representative cross-section of the very real (and oftentimes angst-filled) correspondences that I've received over the past several years—particularly about relationships—via letters, phone calls, consultations, and E-mails. I am grateful to everyone who has contacted my office, and have enjoyed being able to reach out across the miles via the Internet to people I may otherwise never have an opportunity to meet. (For purposes of confidentiality names and specific identifying characteristics have been edited, but the situations, issues, and requests are, to the greatest extent possible, original.)

In sharing these letters and my responses to them, I have attempted to include topics that either were not discussed in the previous chapters, or that were mentioned without as much focus or attention as some readers may desire. It is my hope that you will find guidance through the concerns expressed by other people in their letters. Again, bear in mind that we learn from each other. And, as always, feel free to write to me directly. My Web site and E-mail information are listed in the biography in the back of this book.

> *Dear Dr. Rick,*
>
> *Several years back I began a relationship with a woman. This was the first lesbian relationship I'd ever been in, and during this time I was attending a strict private Baptist college in Mississippi. While in this relationship, I was not out to anyone. I constantly worried about my parents finding out, college expulsion, and religious rejection. Unfortunately, I really let my decisions about the growth of our relationship be directed by my theological convictions.*
>
> *Finally, my girlfriend got tired of my secrets and decided she did not want to continue the deception with me. I decided to believe the hype and marry a man. I would do what everyone said was possible: "Marry and pray to change my evil ways." I married and moved to California. I prayed and found myself more and more unhappy.*
>
> *I left my husband a few years later, left the Baptist faith, and then decided to try again at a more open, honest lesbian relationship. But now I find myself, three years into a happy relationship, again questioning my religious destiny. My question is this: How do I trust myself enough to know that I will be OK? Does my fear about this relationship come from a fear of noncommitment or truly a religious struggle? It's hard to maintain any strong self-esteem, given what my family and society overall have always told me. I want my*

current relationship to last, and I want to find a space
where I no longer have to have SO MUCH guilt. I pray
to go forward.
—*Guilty Gert*

Dear Gert,

You pose powerful questions and issues that I think many
people struggle with to one degree or another: How to accept
who you are and trust your ability to have loving, lasting relationships while battling the continual conflict within—a conflict born of a religious upbringing, deeply ingrained family
beliefs, and societal messages. You are not alone with your fears
and guilt.

It's ironic that religion, to which many people turn in order
to feel better about themselves and their relationship with a
higher power and to feel that they *belong* in this world, can be
such a source of damage to one's self-esteem if one does not fit
the exact mold. And so much of that depends upon specific
interpretations of the Bible (or other religious text). The Baptist
church, of course, is notorious for not accepting gay people.
And many religions are adept at controlling their followers
through guilt and fear.

I do not hear in your letter that you have an issue with
commitment; quite the contrary, you seem very committed
spiritually and indeed are willing to work hard at your relationships. You also state that you want to "move forward,"
free of the guilt that has caused your relationship problems in
the past. The first step forward would be to work through the
messages you've internalized from your family and your
(prior) church. Only when you believe that you are not
wrong/evil/bad/hated by God for being gay will you be free
of the guilt that will accompany any present or future love

relationship. So that's your first order of business: To replace those old, destructive messages with affirming, esteem-enhancing beliefs. It's not an easy task and will require time and patience with yourself, but you'll be facing similar messages your whole life, if not from church or family, from other venues in society, so it's a most worthwhile effort. You express such tremendous pressure (and the resulting stress) to try and live a life that is contrary to who you really are...and it's highly destructive to any effort toward a happy, healthy relationship, as you've discovered.

I strongly recommend that you seek counseling with a therapist familiar with GLBT issues. Also, there are some very good books about homosexuality and the Bible, which you can find at a local bookstore or by doing a search online. And if you are able to meet other gays and lesbians where you live—through organizations, activities, etc.—and begin to develop a support system of like-minded, accepting, supportive people (perhaps with women in particular), you will not only feel less alone, but also experience some community support for your love relationships. That kind of support is important in the nurturing of all our relationships. Best wishes for finding the inner spiritual reconciliation and guidance that will be most helpful, and for maintaining satisfying and rewarding relationships throughout your life.

Dear Dr. Rick,

I've met a fantastic guy and we've been dating for about four months. As I've been single for almost three years now, I'm ready to settle down, but he's just recently out of a decade-long relationship. He tells me he loves me and that I'm more special than the others, but says he wants to be single for a while

*before committing to anyone. I'm afraid I'll lose him
if I hold on too tight, but I also feel like I run the risk
of losing him if I let him go out with so many other
guys. What to do?*
—*Worried in Waltham*

Dear Worried,

You're right: You do run the risk of losing him if you hold
on too tight. He has given you the message that he doesn't want
to be held tightly at this time in his life. And as for letting him
go out with so many other guys, well, that's just not in your
control. If that's what he needs to do, your attempt to deny him
other social or romantic or sexual involvements is not the issue
here, even if it were up to you. That is really a trust issue.

I would ask you this: Why are you dating someone who
desires others, while you desire only him? That's a recipe for
frustration and anxiety for you, which is what you're experiencing now. He may be fantastic in many ways, but being
interested in settling down is not one of them, at least for the
present, and that seems to be what you desire. If you were getting enough of what you need from this relationship then you'd
be happy. But this is not the case. If it continues with him,
you'll have to be satisfied with only the morsels and not the
whole meal until he's ready to see only you. And there's no
guarantee that will happen. Furthermore, telling you that
you're "more special than the others" is like dangling a carrot
in front of you; it may be true, but it's also manipulative since
it keeps you both invested and hopeful.

Ask yourself some hard questions and be fully honest with
your answers: How long am I willing to be involved with someone who is dating others? (Perhaps a time limitation may help
you relax and just enjoy his company whenever he is available.)

Why do I go for men who aren't as available to me as I am to them? (If this is a pattern with you, then you've just identified a self-esteem issue.) Do I deserve to have what I want? (Are there childhood messages connected to this—issues around deservingness and worthiness?) How might I go about finding someone who can offer me the type of commitment I desire?

There are plenty of good men out there who want what you want. But first, you have to be honest and clear with yourself about what it is you truly want, need and are ready for—paying particular attention to that last part: What you are ready for. Then stick to your guns and be true to (and careful with) your heart. It's the only one you have.

Dear Dr. Rick,

I've been seeing someone for about six weeks and we've been practically inseparable since. We are both HIV negative, and I don't have sex with anyone else. He tells me he doesn't either, and I trust him. He has admitted to a history of cheating on lovers in the past, but tells me that's all over now, and I'm the only one for him. I believe him. The real issue for me is that he wants to have unprotected sex. I want to please him, and frankly, I'd ditch the condoms if it's going to be just us. Think that's a bad idea?
—Randy in Ramada Hills

Dear Randy,

Yes, I do. I hate to be cynical, but everyone he cheated on in the past may well have heard those same words: "All that's over now, and you're the only one for me." Please—that sounds like something out of a '40s movie. Six weeks is not a long time, and frankly, I don't think *you're* convinced that he'll be loyal to you. Here's my suggestion: Both of you go get tested at this point in your relationship. Wait a couple more months, then get tested again. All during this time you continue to use condoms. If you're both still HIV negative after the second round of tests, you'll have more of a track record together and perhaps can better determine your level of trust. You'll also know if you can both handle monogamy and wish to proceed without condoms. For the record, though, let me state something important: Even if his (and your) desire is to be monogamous, unless you are genuinely exclusive with each other, using protection is the safest way to go while HIV continues to ravage our planet.

> *Dear Dr. Rick,*
>
> *I have a sister whom I love dearly, but who might as well have been born in another galaxy. That's how different we are. I'm a city gal, she's a suburbanite. She's married with a child, I'm happily single and gay. (Or is it "gaily single?") I love travel and the arts, she would rather go to the mall. In addition, my sister is a super-controlling person who insists on deciding what everyone around her does. This makes family visits difficult. I have a hard time keeping my temper when she's insisted on having her way for the 100th time in a day, yet I hate upsetting my mom, who of course loves us both. Any suggestions for dealing with this behavior?*
> *—Stifled Sister*

Dear Sis,

This is one of those topics to which I referred earlier that isn't just about being gay; it's about something everyone can relate to: family issues.

Families—can't live with them, can't send them all to the

moon. Honest communication is a crucial component in resolving any interpersonal conflict. Perhaps you have some internal block to communicating your feelings toward your sister, so instead you keep trying to hold your temper. That's a sign the situation has really got you frustrated. The more afraid we are that we will blow up, the harder we try to keep the lid on our anger. Where there's anger, there's usually fear one level below. In your case, I'd say your fear is about the destruction your anger might cause—to your relationship with your sister and to your mother.

There are ways to communicate feelings—even difficult or painful feelings—with love and care. Just because we feel angry, doesn't mean we have to express our anger in destructive ways. The next time you are with your sister, consider taking her aside, perhaps spend some one-on-one time with just her, and let her know what happens to you when she's being controlling. Do this *before* you get exasperated. It's important to be gentle, because guess where her controlling behavior is coming from: her *own* fears. If you come from a place of love, you'll be able to explain that you want to reach a resolution together because you value the relationship and love her very much. She doesn't want to be unlikable or the cause of hurt feelings either, but apparently she is unaware of the effects of her controlling behavior on those around her. It may sting at first, and she might not take it well, but in time an even closer relationship will develop as a result of your courage and honesty.

Remember this: *No one ever died from having a feeling.* However, people indeed die or at least develop all sorts of physical disorders—high blood pressure, heart disease, cancer— because they keep their feelings bottled up. Take a breath, then talk about it, whatever "it" is. You'll live longer and happier.

You'll be the model of openness to all your friends and family. And in the process you'll develop honest, mutually rewarding relationships.

> *Dear Dr. Rick,*
>
> *I have a friend at work I feel sure is gay, but he hasn't said anything to me directly. If it were a woman, I would be more comfortable pushing the subject of romance (you know, casually asking if she's seeing anyone), but since he's a man and I'm a woman, it just doesn't feel natural to bring it up in conversation. He's come close to disclosing more about himself, but shies away from mentioning the sex of his "friends." We're just casual friends at the office, and it's not like I expect him to confide his deep dark secrets, but does the fact that he dates men need to be so mysterious? Should I just ask him straight out (as it were)? Or should I respect his privacy even though there's this rather silly black hole in our conversations?*
> *—Curious Coworker*

Dear Curious,

This is a common issue since it illuminates the fine line that many friends of "suspected gay people" struggle with, the line between asking—which, in reality, is a form of outing—and respecting a person's privacy. Even more, this is about respecting a person's *process.*

The male-female dynamic to which you refer may play a role in how you approach him. Some issues may be lurking there for you to explore about yourself. Those issues may or may not matter to *him,* however. If someone feels enough safety, compassion, and openness from others, then personal disclosures tend to be more forthcoming as the level of trust increases, matters of gender aside.

But there are likely other reasons why you don't feel comfortable enough to ask him about his sexual orientation directly. Perhaps you sense something about his need for privacy, or maybe it's about your own comfort level regarding gay folk. Either way, I think you can trust your hunch toward propriety.

I sense that you'd welcome the casual friendship to grow closer, and indeed that does happen as people get to know each other better. What matters to most people is how they *feel* in the company of friends, coworkers, significant others, family, etc. That's what builds trust. What you can do is make sure that you are an open and affirming friend, so that the invitation to disclose, if and when he so wishes and according to *his* own process, is present and felt. And really, that's the kind of friend that's appreciated, gay or straight.

Dear Dr. Rick,

When is the best time and how does one explain homosexuality to children? How detailed should one be regarding actual sex acts? This is an issue that my spouse and I are currently dealing with, as our 6-year-old child has started to ask some questions.

—Pondering Parent

Dear Pondering,

Child development experts generally agree that the time to discuss the birds and the bees with children is when they start asking questions. I see no reason to treat discussions about homosexuality any differently than discussions about heterosexuality, especially if we are to teach our children that there's nothing wrong with being gay. And that's an important point:

More than the facts, children pick up on the *feelings* of those around them. So *how* you teach something is at least as important as the words you are saying. If the topic of homosexuality is natural and comfortable for you, the child will feel that way too. If you're overly anxious, they will sense something's amiss and may shy away from future discussions with you.

Also, 6-year-olds may ask one simple question and then not ask anything again for several years. Maybe they heard a comment at school but are too young to understand what they heard. Keeping your answers equally simple and direct usually satisfies a young child's curiosity. I love the simple definition of homosexuality that a friend of mine once gave to his son: "It's the way some people love."

As the child becomes older, the questions become more specific, and parents need to answer in kind: specifically, directly, honestly. If questions do become about actual sex acts, then again, *how* you answer communicates your attitudes, fears and judgments. Getting in touch with your own relationship to sex is an important ingredient to healthy parenting. Regardless of the age of your child now, you can rest assured the questions are coming. Parents would do well to prepare themselves accordingly.

Here are some tips that may help:

- Answer the question that's asked simply, directly, and honestly.
- Remember you're projecting not just your words but also your attitudes—*especially* your attitudes.
- Prepare yourself by having books in the house to which you and your child can refer. This is particularly helpful when the questions become more complicated.
- Consider having a gay relative or friend available for fur-

ther discussion. A positive role model may assist not only in your child's understanding of facts but would also make an *impression* worth more than any explanation.

- Just because a child asks about homosexuality doesn't mean she or he is going to be gay. (It seems every parent I've ever talked to—gay or straight—is concerned about this, a concern often stemming not so much from a place of prejudice but instead from a parental instinct to ensure a child's happiness and safety and best prepare the child for whatever may lie ahead.) Some of the questions to ask yourself are: What if your child does grow up to be gay? Are you comfortable with—and open to—that? What are your (and your partner's) true beliefs and feelings toward homosexuality?

If your child feels she or he can ask you about sex and receive honest nonjudgmental answers, she or he will come to you with other important questions as well: questions about drugs, drinking, friends, career, and other life issues for which parental guidance may be needed. And if you are available for discussion, no matter what questions they may have, then you are giving your kids a positive message: I care about you, I want you to be an informed, aware, compassionate person, and you can trust me to help however I can.

Such a message sets the stage for a lifelong, healthy, open, and rewarding relationship with your child.

• • •

I receive many letters from gay people about their experiences with coming out to family members. Included among them are many heartwarming tales of love and acceptance.

But for every story of love, there is news of a parent rejecting their son or daughter, either because of homophobic religious beliefs, fear of societal condemnation, or just plain ignorance. I've counseled young people who were literally thrown out of their home and were living on the streets because they disclosed their sexual orientation to the wrong person at the wrong time. I've worked with AIDS patients whose families disowned them for being unapologetically both gay and (homo)sexually active. Two strikes by which the unenlightened cannot abide.

This is why it's so hard for some people to be who they are with honesty and pride, especially in those rural and suburban areas of the country where fear, prejudice, and conservative theology reign supreme. Coming out shouldn't have to be an act of courage, but it is. Being true and genuine to one's nature ought to be applauded, but it's often discouraged and disparaged because of misperceptions, falsehoods, fear, and poor leadership on the part of preachers and politicians alike. To those community leaders, lawmakers, teachers, and family members who understand that diversity is to be celebrated and protected at all costs, I applaud you. To those who reject others—including your own loved ones!—based upon a difference in, and fear of, sexual orientation, I offer the following letter to aid in your understanding and hopefully, to increase your level of empathy.

Dear Mom and Dad,

1. Remember that I need reassurance of your love. The decision to tell you was long and agonizing. I know some parents who have accused, threatened, and rejected their own flesh and blood. Please don't do that to me. Just continue to love me. I'm the same person I was yesterday. You just know more about me today.

2. *"Why? Where did we go wrong? Should we have done something different?"* No one really knows all of what contributes to a person's sexuality, whether gay or straight. You didn't go wrong anywhere; there's nothing you could've done. Don't take responsibility for my being gay. Instead, ask how we can work together in your understanding of me. I need your support, not your guilt.

3. *Aren't I just telling you something that you've known all along, anyway?* Now, together, we can have honesty where before there was deception; closeness where there was distance. They say the truth can set you free. Well, now I'm free to be genuine, loving, proud, confident, creative, and successful. Will you be a part of that, or will we both lose out?

4. *You always hoped I'd marry a nice person someday.* Well, when I bring home my lover, will you be caring and accepting? A successful relationship is important to me, and I could sure use your support and love to help me achieve that.

5. *Lots of lesbians and gay men provide grandchildren for their parents, and lots of heterosexual couples don't.* Let's try not to assume anything about my future or see this as a loss of dreams you may have had for me...or for you.

6. *I've felt alone for too long now.* But that's not necessary anymore for either of us. Please find someone to talk to: a friend, relative, counselor, or someone with PFLAG (Parents, Friends and Families of Lesbians and Gays). I'll help you. We're in this together.

7. *I won't come out only to go back in.* Eventually, I hope you can treat my partner and me with the same love and respect that you'd treat your heterosexual child. This is not something to forget about. We mustn't return to a place of denial. Let's keep communication open. Ask about me. Ask about him or her. It will make all the difference.

There's always more to do in your coming-out process; there's always one more step, one more person to tell. No matter how out you are, make a commitment with yourself to continually allow someone else to know you. In the process you will allow yourself ever more rewarding friendships and relationships, ever more honesty and genuineness in the relationship you develop with yourself. Remember, we all benefit every time the closet door opens a bit wider.

~

To diminish ignorance is to embrace diversity.

~

To erase hate is to embrace love.

Conclusion

A Gay Relationship With God

Don't block the blessing!
—Patti LaBelle

From the moment I walked in, I thought how they looked like a group of people more into partying than praying. There were all kinds of people here: elderly couples, young families, teenagers, groups of gay men, and lesbian couples. And they were all on their feet, singing a lovely hymn at full volume, faces smiling, some with closed eyes. A small, casual, yet enthusiastic and inspirational choir was in the corner, singing their hearts out. Sure, there was a bit of "God" and "Lord" thrown into the lyrics to clue one into the fact that it was a religious gathering, but this was mostly just the general sound of happiness—not at all like most churches I'd visited.

Then everyone sat down, and a young engaging woman with a welcoming style and very short-cropped hair approached the podium in her flowing robe, wished everyone a good morning, and explained that the pamphlet called "Homosexuality and the Bible," which many in the congregation had requested, had come in and would be available in the hall after service.

I thought, *Now, this is my kind of church.*

Richard L. Pimental-Habib, Ph.D.

An Alienating Past

Those of you who have read earlier writings of mine know
that my experience with organized religion is largely based upon
a young life where spirituality meant worshiping at a conservative Catholic altar. My childhood church was one of fiercely dog-
matic, intolerant, and homophobic homilies led by a stern man
with a booming, frightening voice who, even to my young mind,
did not at all represent the God I believed in. By the time I
reached age 16, I was wise enough to know that this environment
did not provide a healthy path for my spiritual or psychological
development. And as a budding young gay boy, I was not about
to accept a religious dogma that didn't accept me. I knew I was
neither hated nor rejected by *my* God; in fact, it was quite clear
in my mind, even as a teenager, that I was as much a part of
God's overall plan as anyone. I knew on some level that I was as
important a piece of the big cosmic picture as any of the sports-
loving, girl-chasing boys with whom I shared weekly catechism
classes. Condemnation and false rhetoric by a hot-aired, hate-
filled priest was not for me.

So, at 16, I left the church to follow my own custom-
designed, evolving spiritual practice, complete with an eclectic
set of beliefs. My journey has led me to explore Eastern philosophy and spirituality as well as more traditional Western
concepts of religion. Jesus Christ is one of my heroes, and so
is Buddha. So is Mahatma Gandhi. Kwanza is one of the most
beautiful celebrations of spirituality on the planet, and I cherish the seders I've enjoyed with my close Reform Jewish
friends. I pray, I meditate. I remember as a young boy the
beauty and pomp of the Mass whenever I attended with my
loving and sometimes mischievous grandmother, who'd let me
eat hard candies in church—an act seriously frowned upon by
the nuns!

Now, my own sense of *belongingness* in relation to the grand cosmos, the big picture—as well as my ever-developing sense of self, both of which are intimately woven into the fabric of my spirituality—is a refection of this synthesis of religious exploration.

A Spiritual Path

So you can imagine how, until I'd reached age 40, I had not found an organized congregation embracing the spiritual values I hold so deeply. What a breath of fresh air to walk into this church and see banners swaying above my head displaying symbols of unity, acceptance, covenant, and the rainbow. I'm still not an advocate of organized religion in general, believing that too often it is detrimental and distracting to the gestalt, the holistic picture of an individual's psychological development. But I couldn't help wonder if I may have found an environment with this church where I could openly be myself, further explore my spiritual growth, and actually feel welcomed and included as a gay man by my fellow worshipers. This was not a "gay church" by any means, but it simply *felt* good.

Certainly, there are churches as well as synagogues and nondenominational places of worship that are gay-founded. Such groups, obviously, are supportive of gay people (as well as nongay people) who are looking for an alternative to traditional settings which they have found to be exclusive and intolerant, much as I have too. I've sampled many of the more progressive denominations over the years and was usually very happy with what I found there. But still, I never felt I could successfully connect on any kind of deep spiritual level at their worship services. Spirituality is such a personal thing to me, that knowing if you've found a place where you want to belong is more a product of intuition than something that is reasoned out. It's much more *felt* than *thought*.

Well, this place felt good: accepting, inclusive, inviting.

I regularly attend this church with my lover, and we are always met with warm smiles, friendly faces, and genuine people who remember both our names. As my lover and I sit together during services, my arm around his shoulder, I feel grounded in the belief that my spiritual path is to be all I am now and to awaken to all I am capable of becoming. And this spiritual conviction is much like what happens in a healthy relationship: I am encouraged to be fully myself and to creatively explore, in the safety of my partner's arms, who I am becoming.

We are all part of the plan—part of all that means godliness, holiness, sacredness, universality, mother earth, father time, creation—whatever terms you wish to use. We are an integral part of what makes it all work. Ancient Eastern wisdom teaches that one cannot so much as touch a flower without there being a chain reaction of connectedness with all other living things, a connectedness that reaches completely around the globe. Each one of us has made the world a certain kind of place for better or worse, and each person, each word, each action affects all of us.

Your presence on this planet matters. Being precisely who you are matters—God's creation, fortes and flaws and all.

As gay, lesbian, bisexual, and transgendered people, we all matter. Yet that is not always the message we receive, especially from the church. Dr. Laura spews forth an insidious and cruel bigotry that claims we are "biological errors," and narrow-thinking, unevolved, noninclusive churches say that we can change if we really want to. Sexual orientation isn't something we decide. We are not mistakes. We are not aberrations. We are not anything less important or sacred or desired by our Creator than anyone else.

Two people who love each other is a wonderful good thing. We are who we are. We love whom we love. As we chant at rallies, "We're here, we're queer, get used to it!"

My Wish for You ...

As we bring to a close this brief journey we have taken together, my wish for you is a lifetime of feeling loved by many different people—people who are good *for* you and good *to* you, including family, friends, and lovers...

That you know the love and companionship of a good partner...

That you know the unconditional acceptance of a dear and lifelong friend...

That you know what it's like to fully love another person without hesitation or restriction or censorship...

That you believe in your own *worthiness* with your whole heart and mind...

That you know, securely and irrevocably, that you are a wonderfully unique and creative work in progress who *belongs*...

And that within your own particular brand of fabulous uniqueness you discover that you are, undeniably and forever, lovable.

I celebrate who I am at this moment and who I am to become along my journey.

~
I seek discovery of myself with joy, love, and acceptance.

~

I embrace my unique and loving spirit.

About the Author

Dr. Richard L. Pimental-Habib, Ph.D., CCH, is a counselor and psychotherapist and holds a doctorate in clinical hypnotherapy with an emphasis in mind/body wellness. His graduate training was in psychodynamic psychotherapy; developmental psychoanalytic psychology; and marriage, family, and child counseling. In recent years he has synthesized meditation, creative visualization, and clinical hypnosis with very encouraging results, especially for patients suffering from life-threatening illnesses.

During his 15-year private practice in Los Angeles, "Dr. Rick" developed a variety of seminars for GLBT empowerment, wellness, and spirituality. He volunteered as a consultant for many HIV and GLBT agencies throughout California and was the bereavement director for the nation's first AIDS hospice. There he designed support programs that continue to serve as models for such institutions nationwide.

Dr. Rick's first book, *Empowering the Tribe: A Positive Guide to Gay and Lesbian Self-Esteem,* was published in 1999. In addition, he's the author of several professional papers on HIV-related grief and grief counseling. He has written for national parenting magazines and has been a regular columnist for several GLBT publications.

Dr. Pimental-Habib now lives with his partner in South Florida along with several overly empowered cats and a very patient dog. Visit his Web site at www.DrRPH.com.